RELATIONSHIPS

LEARNING TO LOVE

	ENTRY LEVEL	ADVANCED LEVEL
SESSION 1 Getting Acquainted	Getting Down to the Basics Genesis 2:18–25	
SESSION 2 Loving God	The Greatest Commandment Mark 12:28–34	Coming Near to God James 4:1–10
SESSION 3 Loving Ourselves	Realizing our Potential Mark 14:27–31,66–72	Children of God 1 John 2:28–3:10
SESSION 4 Loving Family	A Family Conflict Luke 15:11–32	Family Relations Ephesians 5:21–6:4
SESSION 5 Loving Christians	A Life of Service John 13:1–17	Body Support 1 Corinthians 12:12–27
SESSION 6 Loving Non-Christians	Breaking Barriers John 4:4–26	Loving Outsiders Romans 12:9–21
SESSION 7 Loving Our Enemies	Some People Matthew 5:38–48	Paul's Enemies Phil. 1:12–18a,27–2:4

Serendipity House / P.O. Box 1012 / Littleton, CO 80160

TOLL FREE 1-800-525-9563 / www.serendipityhouse.com

00 01 02 / **101 series • CHG** / 6

PROJECT ENGINEER:
Lyman Coleman

WRITING TEAM:
Richard Peace, Lyman Coleman, Matthew Lockhart, Andrew Sloan, Cathy Tardif

PRODUCTION TEAM:
Christopher Werner, Sharon Penington, Erika Tiepel

COVER PHOTO:
© 1998, Comstock, Inc.

CORE VALUES

Community:	The purpose of this curriculum is to build community within the body of believers around Jesus Christ.
Group Process:	To build community, the curriculum must be designed to take a group through a step-by-step process of sharing your story with one another.
Interactive Bible Study:	To share your "story," the approach to Scripture in the curriculum needs to be open-ended and right brain—to "level the playing field" and encourage everyone to share.
Developmental Stages:	To provide a healthy program in the life cycle of a group, the curriculum needs to offer courses on three levels of commitment: (1) Beginner Stage—low-level entry, high structure, to level the playing field; (2) Growth Stage—deeper Bible study, flexible structure, to encourage group accountability; (3) Discipleship Stage—in-depth Bible study, open structure, to move the group into high gear.
Target Audiences:	To build community throughout the culture of the church, the curriculum needs to be flexible, adaptable and transferable into the structure of the average church.

ACKNOWLEDGMENTS

To Zondervan Bible Publishers
for permission to use
the NIV text,
The Holy Bible, New International Bible Society.
© 1973, 1978, 1984 by International Bible Society.
Used by permission of Zondervan Bible Publishers.

Questions and Answers

PURPOSE

1. **What is the purpose of this group?**

   In a nutshell, the purpose is to get acquainted and to double the size of the group.

STAGE

2. **What stage in the life cycle of a small group is this course designed for?**

   This 101 course is designed for the first stage in the three-stage life cycle of a small group. (See diagram below.) For a full explanation of the three-stage life cycle, see the center section.

GOALS

3. **What is the purpose of stage one in the life cycle?**

   The focus in this first stage is primarily on Group Building.

GROUP BUILDING

4. **How does this course develop Group Building?**

   Take a look at the illustration of the baseball diamond on page M5 in the center section. In the process of using this course, you will go around the four bases.

BIBLE STUDY

5. **What is the approach to Bible Study in this course?**

   As shown on page M4 of the center section, there are two tracks in this book. Track 1 is the light option, based on stories in the Bible. Track 2 is the heavier option, based on teaching passages in the Bible.

THREE-STAGE LIFE CYCLE OF A GROUP

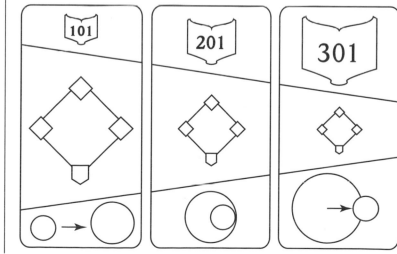

3

6. Which option of Bible Study is best for our group?

Track 1 is the best option for people not familiar with the Bible, as well as for groups who are not familiar with each other. Track 2 is the best option for groups who are familiar with the Bible *and* with one another. (However, whenever you have new people come to a meeting, we recommend you switch to Track 1 for that Bible Study.)

7. Can we choose both options?

Yes, depending upon your time schedule. Here's how to decide:

STUDY	APPROXIMATE COMPLETION TIME
Story Sharing only	60–90 minutes
Epistle Study only	60–90 minutes
Story and Epistle Study	90–120 minutes

8. What if we want to do both the Story and Epistle Studies but don't have time at the session?

You can spend two weeks on a unit—the Story Questionnaire the first week and the Epistle Study the next. Session 1 has only one Bible Study—so you would end up with 13 weeks if you followed this plan.

9. What if you don't know anything about the Bible?

No problem. The Story option is based on a parable or story that stands on its own—to discuss as though you are hearing it for the first time. The Epistle Study comes complete with reference notes—to help you understand the context of the Bible passage and any difficult words that need to be defined.

THE FEARLESS FOURSOME!

If you have more than seven people at a meeting, Serendipity recommends you divide into groups of 4 for the Bible Study. Count off around the group: "one, two, one, two, etc."—and have the "ones" move quickly to another room for the Bible Study. Ask one person to be the leader and follow the directions for the Bible Study time. After 30 minutes, the Group Leader will call "Time" and ask all groups to come together for the Caring Time.

10. **What is the mission of a 101 group?**

Turn to page M5 of the center section. This course is designed for groups in the Birth stage—which means that your mission is to increase the size of the group by filling the "empty chair."

11. **How do we fill the empty chair?**

Pull up an empty chair during the group's prayer time and ask God to bring a new person to the group to fill it.

12. **What is a group covenant?**

A group covenant is a "contract" that spells out your expectations and the ground rules for your group. It's very important that your group discuss these issues—preferably as part of the first session.

13. **What are the ground rules for the group?** (Check those that you agree upon.)

❐ PRIORITY: While you are in the course, you give the group meetings priority.

❐ PARTICIPATION: Everyone participates and no one dominates.

❐ RESPECT: Everyone is given the right to their own opinion and all questions are encouraged and respected.

❐ CONFIDENTIALITY: Anything that is said in the meeting is never repeated outside the meeting.

❐ EMPTY CHAIR: The group stays open to new people at every meeting.

❐ SUPPORT: Permission is given to call upon each other in time of need—even in the middle of the night.

❐ ADVICE GIVING: Unsolicited advice is not allowed.

❐ MISSION: We agree to do everything in our power to start a new group as our mission (see center section).

SESSION

1

Getting Acquainted

3-PART AGENDA

ICE-BREAKER
15 Minutes

BIBLE STUDY
30 Minutes

CARING TIME
15–45 Minutes

Welcome to this course on building better relationships. In this session, we will get an overview of what we will study in the following weeks. Relationships form the foundation of who we are and how we relate to the world around us. Without relationships, life would be uninteresting and dehumanizing. Through our relationships, we learn what it means to be a created human being.

Relationships are not automatically great. Successful relationships with God and with others take work in order to be healthy and strong. They do not just happen. At the center of successful relationships is love and respect. Healthy relationships are marked by equality—both giving and receiving—or else you will find yourself in a codependent relationship. Healthy relationships are balanced and add to our lives. Unhealthy relationships throw our lives off balance.

> **LEADER: Be sure to read the "Questions and Answers" on pages 3–5. Take some time during this first session to have the group go over the ground rules on page 5. At the beginning of the Caring Time have your group look at pages M1–M3 in the center section of this book.**

Along with considering our need for relationships in general, in these sessions we will look at the following relationships in particular:
- our relationship with God
- our relationship with ourselves
- our relationship with family members
- our relationship with those inside the community of faith
- our relationship with those outside the community of faith
- our relationship with our enemies

By examining these relationships, we will discover the important components of relationships and gain skills for developing healthy relationships.

In this course we want to learn about the Bible in a way that sheds light on who we are. The focus, then, will be on telling your story and using the passage as a springboard.

Every session has three parts: (1) **Ice-Breaker**—to break the ice and introduce the topic, (2) **Bible Study**—to share your own life through a passage of Scripture, and (3) **Caring Time**—to share prayer concerns and pray for one another.

Ice-Breaker / 15 Minutes

My Roles. Everyone has many roles in their life. Help your group get to know you better by telling them all the roles in your life.

I AM A ...

❐ Father	❐ Boss	❐ Hobbyist
❐ Mother	❐ Landlord	❐ Homeowner
❐ Brother	❐ Tenant	❐ Auto operator
❐ Sister	❐ Political activist	❐ Small group member
❐ Husband	❐ Taxpayer	❐ Worker
❐ Wife	❐ Church member	❐ Stepparent
❐ Friend	❐ Club member	❐ Stepchild
❐ Pet owner	❐ Student	❐ In-law
❐ Employee	❐ Volunteer	❐ other:_____

Which of these roles is the most fun?

The most challenging?

The most rewarding?

The most frustrating?

Bible Study / 30 Minutes

Genesis 2:18–25 / Getting Down to the Basics

This passage, which is part of the story of Creation, is where all relationships began. Ask one person to read out loud Genesis 2:18–25. Then, share your answers to the following questions. Be sure to save time to discuss the issues in the Caring Time.

[18]*The L*ORD* God said, "It is not good for the man to be alone. I will make a helper suitable for him."*

[19]*Now the L*ORD* God had formed out of the ground all the beasts of the field and all the birds of the air. He brought them to the man to see what he would name them; and whatever the man called each living creature, that was its name.* [20]*So the man gave names to all the livestock, the birds of the air and all the beasts of the field.*

But for Adam no suitable helper was found. [21]*So the L*ORD* God caused the man to fall into a deep sleep; and while he was sleeping, he took one of the man's ribs and closed up the place with flesh.* [22]*Then the L*ORD* God made a woman from the rib he had taken out of the man, and he brought her to the man.*

[23]*The man said,*

> *"This is now bone of my bones*
> *and flesh of my flesh;*
> *she shall be called 'woman,'*
> *for she was taken out of man."*

[24]*For this reason a man will leave his father and mother and be united to his wife, and they will become one flesh.*

[25]*The man and his wife were both naked, and they felt no shame.*

1. Where was your "Garden of Eden" as a child—the place you went to where everything seemed peaceful and harmonious?
   - ❐ my room
   - ❐ my church
   - ❐ a friend's house
   - ❐ a special place outside
   - ❐ my grandparents' home
   - ❐ a secret hideaway
   - ❐ I didn't have such a place.
   - ❐ other: _____

2. Why didn't God make Adam and Eve at the same time?
   - ❐ to demonstrate that people aren't complete when isolated
   - ❐ to help Adam appreciate his new companion
   - ❐ to establish Adam as the leader in their relationship
   - ❐ to save the best for last

3. If you are *single*: How does this story make you feel?
   - ❐ It reinforces the stigma that I can't be complete without a spouse.
   - ❐ It reassures me that it's normal to need companionship.
   - ❐ It confirms that God is in control of my life and relationships.
   - ❐ It convinces me that God doesn't want me to be lonely.

4. If you are *married*: Which of the following are you most grateful for in your marriage? Which would you like to focus on for growth?
   - ❐ our mutual help and support
   - ❐ the companionship we share
   - ❐ the sizzle of our romance
   - ❐ the intimacy of our relationship

5. Which of the following best describes how you feel about relating to other people?
- ❏ "The more people I meet, the more I like my dog."
- ❏ "I love humanity—it's people I can't stand!"
- ❏ "I never met a man (or woman) I didn't like."
- ❏ "People who need people are the luckiest people in the world."
- ❏ "No man (or woman) is an island, apart to himself (or herself)."
- ❏ other:_____

6. How do you feel about spending time alone?
- ❏ I relish those times, and need more of them.
- ❏ I hate those times, and want less of them.
- ❏ Spending time alone is just as important as spending time with others.
- ❏ I need to be careful that I don't spend too much time alone.
- ❏ other:_____

7. Describe a time in your life when you were so lonely that you learned the truth of God's statement, "It is not good ... to be alone" (v. 18).

8. Which type of relationship mentioned in this story do you have the greatest difficulty with?
- ❏ my relationship to God
- ❏ my relationship to animals and the natural world
- ❏ my relationship to the opposite sex
- ❏ my relationship to my parents (or my spouse's parents)

9. In verse 25 we are told that the man and woman were naked before each other, and in their innocent stato (before sin) they felt no shame. What does this say to you, if you are to have better rela-tionshlps?
- ❏ I need to stand "spiritually naked" before people.
- ❏ I need to be in a group where others aren't afraid to stand "spiritually naked" before each other.
- ❏ I can't be ashamed of who I am if I am to relate to others.
- ❏ I need to stop being ashamed of my family members.
- ❏ I need to stop being ashamed of my friends.
- ❏ other:_____

"We are born helpless. As soon as we are fully conscious we discover loneliness. We need others physically, emotionally, intellectually, we need them if we are to know anything, even ourselves."
—C. S. Lewis

Caring Time / 15–45 Minutes

LEADER:
Ask the group, "Who are you going to invite next week?"

The most important time in every meeting is this—the Caring Time—where you take time to share prayer requests and pray for one another. To make sure this time is not neglected, you need to set a minimum time that you will devote to prayer requests and prayer and count backward from the closing time by this amount. For instance, if you are going to close at 9 p.m., and you are going to devote 30 minutes to prayer requests and prayer, you need to ask a timekeeper to call "time" at 8:30 and move to prayer requests. Start out by asking everyone to answer this question:

"How can we help you in prayer this week?"

Then, move into prayer. If you have not prayed out loud before, finish these sentences:

"Hello, God, this is ... (first name). I want to thank you for ..."

Be sure to pray for the "empty chair" (see page M5 in the center section). And as you do, think about who you could invite to join you as you begin this study.

GROUP DIRECTORY

P.S.
At the close, pass around your books and have everyone sign the Group Directory inside the front cover.

SESSION

2

Loving God

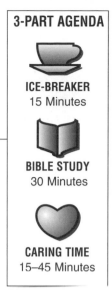

3-PART AGENDA

ICE-BREAKER
15 Minutes

BIBLE STUDY
30 Minutes

CARING TIME
15–45 Minutes

Our relationship with God is the most important relationship in our lives. God is the one who created us from the dust of the earth, breathed life into us, redeemed us from our sins and sustains us throughout life. You may have heard the acronym JOY— Jesus, Others and You, for how we are to prioritize our relationships.

What does it mean to love God? Many of us were taught as children to "Love the Lord your God with all your heart and with all your soul and with all your mind. This is the first and greatest commandment." We are to love God unconditionally and totally. We are to love God more than we love anyone else. We are to love God completely. But the question remains—*how* do we love God?

Jesus answered this in a discussion with his disciples: "If you love me you will obey what I command." Or as the apostle John later wrote, "This is the love of God, that we keep his commandments." The answer to the question is also very similar to how we love others. The way in which we develop a relationship with others is the way we love and develop a relationship with God. We can only know God by spending time with God. J. I. Packer in his book, *Knowing God*, wrote that there is a big difference between "knowing God and knowing about God."

> **LEADER: If there are new people in this session, review the ground rules for this group on page 5. Have the group look at page M4 in the center section and decide which Bible Study option to use— light or heavy. If you have more than seven people, see the box about the "Fearless Foursome" on page 4.**

In order to know God, we need to spend time with God studying his Word and praying—talking with God. But prayer also involves listening for God to speak to us as well. We also get to know God through worship and fellowship with other believers. And the key to loving God is obeying his commandments.

In this session, we will be looking at the ways we can know God and develop a relationship with him. In the Option 1 Study (from the Gospel of Mark), we will consider a passage where Jesus states the greatest commandment. In the Option 2 Study (from James' letter), we will look at what James has to say about our relationship with God and how it influences other relationships.

Ice-Breaker / 15 Minutes

Spiritual Roots. Use the following questions to help your group get to know more about your spiritual roots. Have one person at a time briefly share their answers to the three questions below.

1. When did God become more than just a name to you?

2. Who is the person who shaped and influenced your early spiritual development the most?

❒ my mother   ❒ a close friend
❒ my father   ❒ a neighbor
❒ my brother or sister   ❒ a coach
❒ a grandparent   ❒ a teacher
❒ another relative   ❒ a pastor
❒ a Sunday school teacher   ❒ a youth leader
❒ a scoutmaster or club leader   ❒ other:_____

3. What is something important that person taught you?

Bible Study / 30 Minutes

Option 1 / Gospel Study

Mark 12:28–34 / The Greatest Commandment

Read Mark 12:28–34, and discuss the questions that follow with your group. Religious leaders of Jesus' day spent much time debating the Old Testament Law, and the question of which of the many commandments in Scripture was the greatest probably came up many times. Here we see Jesus' answer.

28One of the teachers of the law came and heard them debating. Noticing that Jesus had given them a good answer, he asked him, "Of all the commandments, which is the most important?"

29"The most important one," answered Jesus, "is this: 'Hear, O Israel, the Lord our God, the Lord is one. 30Love the Lord your God with all your heart and with all your soul and with all your mind and with all your strength.' 31The second is this: 'Love your neighbor as yourself.' There is no commandment greater than these."

32"Well said, teacher," the man replied. "You are right in saying that God is one and there is no other but him. 33To love him with all your heart, with all your understanding and with all your strength, and to love your neighbor as yourself is more important than all burnt offerings and sacrifices."

34When Jesus saw that he had answered wisely, he said to him, "You are not far from the kingdom of God." And from then on no one dared ask him any more questions.

1. From what you see in this passage, how would you describe the relationship between Jesus and this man?
   ❐ argumentative   ❐ respectful
   ❐ affirming   ❐ combative
   ❐ cautious   ❐ mutually probing
   ❐ competitive   ❐ emotionally distant
   ❐ intellectual   ❐ in process

2. What attitude did you have as an adolescent about "debating" the rules?
   ❐ I didn't have any desire to debate them.
   ❐ I didn't have the courage to debate them.
   ❐ I debated them—but always lost the debate.
   ❐ I debated them often—and occasionally won.
   ❐ I debated them constantly—and generally won.
   ❐ I often debated them and won, but wish I would have lost.
   ❐ other:_____

3. Why were people debating the rules and laws with Jesus?
   ❐ Nobody had written them down.
   ❐ They were trying out for the debate team.
   ❐ They liked intellectual exercises.
   ❐ They were trying to find loopholes so they could do what they wanted.
   ❐ They were just trying to get the best of Jesus.
   ❐ These were important things, and they really wanted to know.

13

4. What did Jesus mean when he said to the man, "You are not far from the kingdom of God" (v. 34)?
   ❏ The kingdom of God was coming soon and he would be a part of it
   ❏ The man still had a little growing to do before he could enter the kingdom of God.
   ❏ He had the right ideas—now he had to develop the right relationship with God.
   ❏ other:_____

5. Which of the following reflects your view of God when you were in grade school?
   ❏ a kindly old man—like Santa Claus
   ❏ like my parents
   ❏ like Jesus—I saw God and Jesus as the same.
   ❏ a spirit like Casper the friendly ghost
   ❏ an angry man sending lightning bolts and punishing people
   ❏ I had no concept of God.
   ❏ other:_____

> "God created man because God loves and wanted an object to love. He created man so that he could return his love."
> —Billy Graham

6. How has your view of God changed? Now I view God as:
   ❏ a judge—determined and declaring right and wrong
   ❏ the Creator—powerful, but not very personal
   ❏ a loving father or parent—bringing warmth and intimacy
   ❏ a provider—taking care of all my needs
   ❏ other:_____

7. How are you doing right now at loving God in the ways we are commanded to?

   WITH ALL YOUR HEART: making the relationship heartfelt, instead of merely intellectual

1	2	3	4	5	6	7	8	9	10
I'm a wipeout.				I'm struggling.					I'm on target.

   WITH ALL YOUR SOUL: with total spiritual devotion, disciplining yourself through prayer and reflection

1	2	3	4	5	6	7	8	9	10
I'm a wipeout.				I'm struggling.					I'm on target.

   WITH ALL YOUR MIND: by learning all you can about God's Word and God's will

1	2	3	4	5	6	7	8	9	10
I'm a wipeout.				I'm struggling.					I'm on target.

   WITH ALL YOUR STRENGTH: by giving your time and energy to God's work

1	2	3	4	5	6	7	8	9	10
I'm a wipeout.				I'm struggling.					I'm on target.

8. What do you need to do to love God more fully?
   ❑ learn more about God through personal Bible study, church, and groups like this
   ❑ let God touch my heart more fully
   ❑ give more of my time and energy to God's work
   ❑ love God through loving my "neighbor"
   ❑ other:_____

Option 2 / Epistle Study

James 4:1–10 / Coming Near to God

James discusses how to have a closer relationship with God and be at peace with those around us. Read James 4:1–10 and share your responses to the following questions with your group. The reference notes on pages 17–19 will help you better understand the passage.

4 *What causes fights and quarrels among you? Don't they come from your desires that battle within you?* [2] *You want something but don't get it. You kill and covet, but you cannot have what you want. You quarrel and fight. You do not have, because you do not ask God.* [3] *When you ask, you do not receive, because you ask with wrong motives, that you may spend what you get on your pleasures.*

[4] *You adulterous people, don't you know that friendship with the world is hatred toward God? Anyone who chooses to be a friend of the world becomes an enemy of God.* [5] *Or do you think Scripture says without reason that the spirit he caused to live in us envies intensely?* [6] *But he gives us more grace. That is why Scripture says:*

> *"God opposes the proud*
> *but gives grace to the humble."*

[7] *Submit yourselves, then, to God. Resist the devil, and he will flee from you.* [8] *Come near to God and he will come near to you. Wash your hands, you sinners, and purify your hearts, you double-minded.* [9] *Grieve, mourn and wail. Change your laughter to mourning and your joy to gloom.* [10] *Humble yourselves before the Lord, and he will lift you up.*

1. Who were you most likely to have "fights and quarrels" with when you were in junior high?

2. According to verses 1–3, what is at the root of fights and quarrels? What are the reasons we don't have what we want?

3. What desires do you have that sometimes lead to quarrels with other people?
❏ my desire for control
❏ my desire for what other people have
❏ my desire to be right
❏ my desire to avoid change
❏ other:_____

4. What happens to relationships when we covet?

5. What is God's attitude toward the proud and toward the humble (vv. 6,10)?

6. What is your biggest obstacle to humbling yourself before the Lord? How hard is it for you to submit to God, as opposed to following the ways of the world?

7. Are Christians supposed to look like verse 9? When is this behavior right and necessary (see note on v. 9)?

8. How "near" do you feel to God right now? How does that compare to six months or a year ago?

9. Which of the actions in verses 7–10 impress you the most as something you need to do in your relationship with God?

"The world is a net; the more we stir in it, the more we are entangled."
—Proverb

Caring Time / 15–45 Minutes

Take time at the close to share any personal prayer requests. Answer the question:

"How can we help you in prayer this week?"

Then go around and let each person pray for the person on their right. Finish this sentence:

"Dear God, I want to speak to you about my friend _____."

During your prayer time, remember to pray for the empty chair and for the growth of your group.

LEADER:
Ask the group, "Who are you going to invite next week?"

Reference Notes

Summary. This is the third and final part of James' discussion about wisdom. Here he applies his insights to the question of their community life together as a church. Their failure to live out God's wisdom has had the most serious consequences for them as a church.

4:1–3 James begins by naming the root cause of all this strife. It is the desire for pleasure.

4:1 *What causes fights and quarrels among you?* Where does all this strife come from? It is not initiated by the wise leaders who are peacemakers (James 3:18). It is not caused by persecution from the world. James is very clear that the strife is internal ("among you").

fights and quarrels. Literally, "wars and battles." These are long-term conflicts, not sudden explosions.

desires. Literally, "pleasures." In Greek the word is *hedone,* from which our word "hedonism" is derived. James is not saying that personal pleasure is inherently wrong. However, there is a certain desire for gratification that springs from the wrong source and possesses a person in the pursuit of its fulfillment.

battle. The human personality is pictured as having been invaded by an alien army. "Human nature is indeed in the grip of an overwhelming army of occupation. Its natural aim, it can be truthfully said, is pleasure; and when we consider the amount of time, energy, money, interest and enthusiasm that men and women give to the satisfaction of this aim we can appreciate the accuracy of James' diagnosis; and Christians can use it as a reliable yardstick by which to measure the sincerity of their religion. Is God or pleasure the dominant concern of their life?" (Tasker).

within you. The struggle is within a person—between the part of him or her which is controlled by the Holy Spirit and that which is controlled by the world.

4:2 *You want something.* This is desire at work (see James 1:14).

but don't get it. This is desire frustrated.

kill and covet. This is how frustrated desire responds. It lashes out at others in anger and abuse. (This is "killing" in a metaphorical sense—see Matt. 5:21–22.) It responds in jealousy to those who have what it wants.

quarrel and fight. But still they do not have what they desire so the hostile action continues. This mad desire-driven quest causes a person to disregard other people, trampling over them if necessary to get what they want.

you do not ask God. One reason for this frustrated desire is a lack of prayer.

4:3 James senses a protest: "But I did ask God and I didn't get it." So he qualifies the absolute assertion in verse 2. The desire expressed in prayer may be inappropriate. God will not grant this type of request. Christians pray "in the name of Jesus," implying submission to the will of God. They can ask for wisdom and always expect to get it (if they do not waver), as James explains in 1:5. But this is different than asking for something to sate an illicit pleasure and expecting to get it. Prayer is not magic. The implication is not that God will not give us things that give us pleasure (see Phil. 4:12). The point is that they are motivated by selfish desires and ask simply to gratify themselves. This is not the trusting child asking for a meal but the greedy child asking for the best piece or the spoiled child demanding his or her way. They are asking God to bless their schemes; God will have no part of it (Davids, GNC).

spend. This is the same word used in Luke 15:14 to describe the profligate behavior of the prodigal son.

4:4 *adulterous people.* In Greek, this word is feminine, *adulteresses*, and probably refers to the people of Israel. By extension it refers to the church, the new Israel. In the Old Testament it was common to picture the relationship between God and his people as similar to the relationship between a husband and his wife (Isa. 54:5). To give spiritual allegiance to another ("the world") is therefore expressed in terms of adultery.

4:6 But their case is not hopeless. God does give grace. Repentance is possible. They can turn from their misbehavior.

proud. Haughty and arrogant, to set oneself above others.

grace. To receive grace, a person must *ask* for it. To be able to ask, one must see the need to do so. The proud person can't and doesn't see such a need. Only the humble do.

4:7–10 By means of a series of 10 commands, James tells them how to repent. He has switched to the imperative voice: "Do this," he says, "and you will escape the mess you have gotten yourselves in." Thus he tells them to submit, resist, come near, wash, purify, grieve, mourn, wail, change, and humble themselves.

4:7 *Submit yourselves, then, to God.* His first and primary command is that they must submit to God. It is not too surprising that James says this, since what these Christians have been doing is resisting God and his ways. As James just pointed out, it is the humble who receive God's grace. A proud person is unwilling to submit and therefore not open to grace, feeling that he or she needs nothing.

Resist the devil. Submission to God begins with resistance to Satan. Thus far they have been giving in to the devil's enticements. A clear sign of their new lifestyle will be this inner resistance to devilish desires.

he will flee from you. Since Satan has no ultimate power over a Christian, when resisted he can do little but withdraw.

4:8 Wash your hands. Originally this was a ritual requirement whereby one became ceremoniously clean in preparation for the worship of God (see Ex. 30:19–21). Now it is a symbol of the sort of inner purity God desires.

sinners. Those whose lives have become more characteristic of the enemy than of God—lapsed or "worldly" Christians.

double-minded. This is the parallel word to "sinners" and expresses nicely what life with two competing masters is like. God asks for single-ness of purpose in His disciples.

4:9 mourn and wail. When people realize that they have been leading self-centered lives, in disobedience to God and harmful to others, they often feel overwhelming grief.

4:10 Humble. This last command urges humility before God as did the first command ("Submit to God").

GROUP DIRECTORY

P.S.
If you have a new person in your group, be sure to add their name to the group directory inside the front cover.

Loving Ourselves

3-PART AGENDA

ICE-BREAKER
15 Minutes

BIBLE STUDY
30 Minutes

CARING TIME
15–45 Minutes

Loving ourselves does not imply an ego-centered reality like the old witch in *Snow White*. She reveled in the process of gazing into her mirror and asking, "Mirror, mirror on the wall, who is the fairest one of all?" Loving oneself does mean a genuine caring, concern, and respect for oneself. To care about oneself is basic to love. Humans love themselves when they clearly see themselves and genuinely appreciate what they see. But they are especially excited and challenged with the prospect of what they can become. To love ourselves we must discover and celebrate our uniqueness. And this includes living up to our potential. Herbert Otto says only about five percent of our human potential is realized in our lifetime. What about the other 95 percent?

> **LEADER: If there are more than seven people at this meeting, divide into groups of 4 for Bible Study. Count off around the group: "one, two, one, two, etc."—and have the "ones" quickly move to another room. When you come back together for the Caring Time, have the group read about your Mission on page M5 of the center section.**

Loving yourself involves the knowledge that only you can be you. If you try to be like anyone else, you may come very close, but you will always be second best. But, *you* are the best you. It is the easiest, most practical, most rewarding thing to be. Then it makes sense that you can only be to others what you are to yourself. Leo Buscaglia writes, "If you know, accept and appreciate yourself and your uniqueness, you will permit others to do so. ... To the extent to which you know yourself, and we are all more alike than different, you can know others. When you love yourself, you will love others. And to the depth and extent to which you can love yourself, only to that extent and depth will you be able to love others."

In Option 1, we will study the story of Peter's denial and his need to accept himself for who he really was. In accepting his failures, he could love himself as Christ loved him. And in Option 2, we will study a passage from John's first epistle, where he explains the relationship between loving God and loving ourselves.

Ice-Breaker / 15 Minutes

Self-Affirmation. We all need a pat on the back from time to time. Sometimes we need to pat ourselves on the back—not in a boastful or arrogant way, but as a means of affirming who we are. Choose one or two of the following and share your responses with the group:

❐ Two things I like about my appearance are ...
❐ Two things I do to keep myself healthy are ...
❐ Two jobs I do very well at work are ...
❐ One thing my family appreciates about me is ...
❐ One thing I do to maintain a good friendship is ...
❐ One positive thing others have said about me is ...

Bible Study / 30 Minutes

Option 1 / Gospel Study

Mark 14:27–31,66–72 / Realizing Our Potential

The first part of this story occurs just after the Last Supper. Jesus knows he is about to be arrested; he also knows that his disciples will desert him. When Jesus was arrested, Peter followed at a distance. We pick up the story again as Peter is in the courtyard of the high priest's home, where Jesus is being interrogated. Read Mark 14:27–31,66–72 and discuss your responses to the following questions with the group.

27"You will all fall away," Jesus told them, "for it is written:

> *" 'I will strike the shepherd,*
> > *and the sheep will be scattered.'*

28But after I have risen, I will go ahead of you into Galilee."

29Peter declared, "Even if all fall away, I will not."

30"I tell you the truth," Jesus answered, "today—yes, tonight—before the rooster crows twice you yourself will disown me three times."

31But Peter insisted emphatically, "Even if I have to die with you, I will never disown you." And all the others said the same. ...

66While Peter was below in the courtyard, one of the servant girls of the high priest came by. 67When she saw Peter warming himself, she looked closely at him.

"You also were with that Nazarene, Jesus," she said.

68But he denied it. "I don't know or understand what you're talking about," he said, and went out into the entryway.

[69]*When the servant girl saw him there, she said again to those standing around, "This fellow is one of them."* [70]*Again he denied it.*

After a little while, those standing near said to Peter, "Surely you are one of them, for you are a Galilean."

[71]*He began to call down curses on himself, and he swore to them, "I don't know this man you're talking about."*

[72]*Immediately the rooster crowed the second time. Then Peter remembered the word Jesus had spoken to him: "Before the rooster crows twice you will disown me three times." And he broke down and wept.*

1. Imagine that you were a reporter for *The Jerusalem Journal*, and you were assigned to interview Peter after these events. What would be the first question you would ask him?
   ❒ "So, Peter, how does it feel to be a traitor?"
   ❒ "Didn't you ever think about Jesus' prediction?"
   ❒ "How could you have done such a thing?"
   ❒ "How has this changed the way you see yourself?"
   ❒ "What do you plan to do now to make up for this?"
   ❒ other:_____

2. What is your reaction to Peter's denial of Jesus?
   ❒ I probably would have done the same thing.
   ❒ He was a coward.
   ❒ I pity him.
   ❒ I can't believe he would do something that dumb.
   ❒ I'm angry at him.
   ❒ other:_____

3. In spite of knowing Peter's faults in general and that Peter would deny him, why do you think Jesus chose Peter and changed his name from Simon ("sinking sand") to Peter ("the rock")?
   ❒ Peter was the best man available.
   ❒ Jesus believed in positive thinking.
   ❒ Jesus believed that despite his flaws, Peter would do fine.
   ❒ Jesus wanted to illustrate the power of God.
   ❒ Jesus knew Peter's potential better than Peter did himself.
   ❒ Jesus saw Peter's heart.

4. What impact do you think this failure had on Peter's future?
   ❒ It probably made him less cocky.
   ❒ It probably took away all his self-confidence.
   ❒ It probably made him a more sensitive person.
   ❒ It probably helped to make him into the man of God he became.

5. How do you usually react when you fail?
   ❏ kick myself for days   ❏ hide my feelings
   ❏ try to make up for it   ❏ pray about it
   ❏ admit it and move on   ❏ shrug it off
   ❏ talk to someone about it   ❏ other:_____
   ❏ I refuse to accept failure in anything I do!

6. How has failure changed you?
   ❏ I'm more caring and understanding.
   ❏ I'm more determined.
   ❏ I'm more humble.
   ❏ I'm more realistic.
   ❏ I don't want to try again.
   ❏ I look out for myself more.
   ❏ I'm emotionally fragile.
   ❏ other:_____

7. How do you usually feel about yourself with respect to each of the areas listed below? Mark an **"X"** on the following scale:

   MY PHYSICAL SELF:
   I feel great. _____ _____I don't like myself.

   MY SOCIAL SELF:
   I feel great. _____I don't like myself.

   MY EMOTIONAL SELF:
   I feel great _____I don't like myself.

   MY INTELLECTUAL SELF:
   I feel great. _____I don't like myself.

   MY SPIRITUAL SELF:
   I feel great. _____I don't like myself.

8. This wasn't the end of the story for Peter. After Jesus rose from the dead he appeared to Peter and assured Peter of his love and forgiveness (John 21). What would you need to do to show the same grace toward yourself that Jesus showed to Peter?
   ❏ cut myself a break
   ❏ treat myself to something special
   ❏ ask Christ for forgiveness
   ❏ forgive myself
   ❏ show myself some kindness
   ❏ nothing—I feel great about myself.
   ❏ other:_____

1 John 2:28–3:10 / Children of God

The apostle John emphasized loving others above all other teaching, and showed how loving God was integrally related to loving others. However, in the following passage, he also writes about how God's love for us gives us a status that helps us to love ourselves. Read 1 John 2:28–3:10, and discuss the questions which follow with your group.

> *²⁸And now, dear children, continue in him, so that when he appears we may be confident and unashamed before him at his coming.*
>
> *²⁹If you know that he is righteous, you know that everyone who does what is right has been born of him.*
>
> **3** *How great is the love the Father has lavished on us, that we should be called children of God! And that is what we are! The reason the world does not know us is that it did not know him. ²Dear friends, now we are children of God, and what we will be has not yet been made known. But we know that when he appears, we shall be like him, for we shall see him as he is. ³Everyone who has this hope in him purifies himself, just as he is pure.*
>
> *⁴Everyone who sins breaks the law; in fact, sin is lawlessness. ⁵But you know that he appeared so that he might take away our sins. And in him is no sin. ⁶No one who lives in him keeps on sinning. No one who continues to sin has either seen him or known him.*
>
> *⁷Dear children, do not let anyone lead you astray. He who does what is right is righteous, just as he is righteous. ⁸He who does what is sinful is of the devil, because the devil has been sinning from the beginning. The reason the Son of God appeared was to destroy the devil's work. ⁹No one who is born of God will continue to sin, because God's seed remains in him; he cannot go on sinning, because he has been born of God. ¹⁰This is how we know who the children of God are and who the children of the devil are: Anyone who does not do what is right is not a child of God; nor is anyone who does not love his brother.*

1. Whose coming would motivate you to get busy and clean house? Your boss? Your in-laws? Your small group?

2. What kind of feeling would you have if Jesus Christ returned right now? Excited? Relieved? Ashamed?

3. What is necessary for a person to be "confident and unashamed" at Christ's return (2:28)?

4. What tell-tale attitudes and actions characterize a person "born of God" (2:29; 3:3,6,7,10)?

5. Who is it hardest for you to love—God, other people, or yourself?

6. What do verses 3:1–2 do for your self-image? How does it make you feel to know that followers of Christ one day "shall be like him"?

7. How easy is it for you to see God as your loving Father? How have you experienced God's lavish love recently?

8. Why did Jesus "appear" in the first place (3:5)? How does this make you feel about Jesus? How does this make you feel about yourself?

9. As you get older, do you find the old sinful desires easier or harder to resist? How does this passage of Scripture give you hope?

Caring Time / 15–45 Minutes

Take some time to share any personal prayer requests and answer the question:

"How do you most need God's help in your life right now?"

Close with a short time of prayer, remembering the requests that have been shared. If you would like to pray in silence, say the word "Amen" when you have finished your prayer, so that the next person will know when to start.

Reference Notes

2:28–3:3 Previously, John urged his readers to resist the proselytizing of the false teachers and to remain in Christ. In these verses he continues to urge his readers to remain in Christ, but now the reason he gives has to do with the second coming of Christ. If they remain in Christ, when they meet the Lord at the Second Coming they will not be ashamed. Instead, they will be confident before the Lord (2:28). Furthermore, they know that they will see Christ as he is and be made like him (3:2). The Second Coming is thus a source of great hope for the Christian and an encouragement to holy living (3:3).

2:28 *continue.* The word translated here as "continue" is the same Greek word that was translated "remain" in 2:19,24,27. It can be translated in a variety of ways: "to abide," "to remain steadfast," "to dwell," "to rest," "to persist," "to persevere," or "to be intimately united to." However, the best rendering is "to remain" or "to abide in."

confident and unashamed. On the Day of Judgment (which will occur at the Second Coming), those who have rejected Christ will feel a sense of unworthiness and shame in the presence of his holiness (Isa. 6:5), and because of their open disgrace at having rejected Christ. In contrast, Christians will be able boldly to approach the royal presence because they have lived their lives in union with Christ.

2:29 *everyone who does what is right.* One consequence of spiritual rebirth is right living. It is, in fact, a sign of rebirth as the child begins to display the characteristics of his or her heavenly Father.

born of him. Christians are those who experience "spiritual rebirth." John thus defines the relationship between the believer and God by means of the analogy of the relationship between a child and a father (see also Titus 3:5; 1 Peter 1:3,23).

3:1 The precise nature of what Christians will become when they meet Christ is not fully clear ("what we will be has not yet been made known"). Yet they can get an idea of what they will be like by looking at Jesus ("we shall be like him"). In some way, Christians will become like Jesus when the process of glorification—which began at rebirth—is completed at the Second Coming.

3:3 *this hope.* Namely, that one day Christ will appear again at which time they will see him as he really is and be changed so as to become like him.

pure. This is a common word in the Bible denoting the outward purity required of those persons or objects involved in temple worship. In the usage here it speaks of the moral purity (freedom from sinning) that is required of Christians. Such purification is necessary for those who are in union with Christ.

3:4–10 Having stated that those who are Christians have the hope of the Second Coming as their motivation for purifying themselves, John next looks at the sin from which they must purify themselves. In these verses he addresses the negative: the children of God must not sin. In 3:11–24 he will address the positive: instead, the children of God are to love one another.

3:5 John gives yet another reason for not sinning. The very purpose for Jesus to come in the first place was to take away sin. So it is obvious that Jesus stands over against sin. Furthermore, there was no sin in Jesus' life. The implication is that those who are in union with Christ will reflect this same abhorrence of sin.

in him is no sin. John asserts that Jesus was sinless. His testimony is all the more powerful since this is not his main point. John is not trying to prove anything. He is simply stating what he knows to be true. And John was in a position to know whether Jesus was actually without sin because he lived with Jesus for some three years. Those who live with us know us best. Yet John says—after having seen Jesus in a variety of situations over a three-year period—that Jesus is *without sin.*

3:6 John appears to be saying here (and in vv. 8–10) that a Christian *cannot sin.* Yet in other passages, he points out that Christians can and do sin (e.g., 1:8,10; 2:1; 5:16). Some scholars feel that what John has in mind here is willful and deliberate sin (as against involuntary error). Other scholars stress the tense of the verb that John uses: a Christian does not *keep* on sinning. In other words, Christians do not habitually sin. Still other scholars feel that what John does here is to point out the ideal. This is what would happen if a Christian abided constantly in Christ. In any case, "John is arguing the incongruity rather than the impossibility of sin in the Christian" (Stott).

3:8–10 In these verses John restates what he has said in verses 4–7. This statement parallels his previous statement except that here the focus is on the origin of sin (it is of the devil) rather than on the nature of sin (it is breaking the Law).

3:8 sinful. In verse 4, sinfulness was described as lawbreaking. Here sin is linked with Satan who from the beginning has sinned.

of the devil. Just as Christians display their Father's nature by moral living, so too others demonstrate by their immoral lifestyles that Satan is really their father.

3:9 God's seed. John probably is referring either to the Word of God (see Luke 8:11; James 1:18; 1 Peter 1:23) or to the Holy Spirit (see John 3:6) or to both, by which the Christian is kept from sin. In any case, "seed" is a metaphor for the indwelling power of God which brings forth new life.

cannot go on sinning. In 1:8,10 and 2:1, John attacks those who deny that they are sinners in need of forgiveness (i.e., those who are blind to the fact of their sin). Yet here he seems to say that Christians cannot sin. Some scholars feel that in chapter one John was responding to one aspect of the pre-Gnostic heresy of the false teachers—i.e., their teaching that those who were spiritually enlightened were perfect. But here he is dealing with a second aspect of that heresy—i.e., the teaching that sin did not matter. To those holding the first view he declared the universality of sin (all are sinners). Here, in the face of the second error, he declares the incompatibility of sin with the Christian life.

SESSION

4

Loving Family

3-PART AGENDA

ICE-BREAKER
15 Minutes

BIBLE STUDY
30 Minutes

CARING TIME
15–45 Minutes

Let's admit it—at times the most difficult people to love are family members. On the surface we say that we love them, because that is what is expected of us. However, there are simply some people whose personalities "rub us the wrong way." If we met those persons at a company picnic or at the grocery store, we could avoid them. However, if we meet them at a family dinner, there is little that we can do. "You can pick your friends, but you can't pick your family." Deep down, some family members may be extremely difficult to love. Perhaps they have disappointed us or hurt us. Because of the closeness of the relationships, we usually feel the pain more deeply when we are hurt by a family member.

> **LEADER: If you have a new person at this session, remember to use Option 1 rather than Option 2 for the Bible Study. During the Caring Time, don't forget to keep praying for the empty chair.**

Even the most loving families experience friction when people live under the same roof. Some of this conflict is usually just light banter and produces little hostility or pain. The strains and trials of keeping a marriage healthy, raising children, and making ends meet combine to make fertile soil for family conflict.

While family conflict is inevitable, it does not have to blow a family apart. Through loving patience and understanding, conflict can actually strengthen a loving family relationship. Communication is the key. Solutions to conflict can usually be found when members are able to freely talk and listen without being devastated. Sometimes, however, outside help is needed, and a family should feel free to call on a minister or a professional counselor when necessary.

In the following Option 1 Study (from Luke's Gospel), we will see a son's rebellion and a father's pain turn into a tearful reunion. And in Option 2 (from Paul's letter to the Ephesians), we will see how Paul addresses the relationships of husbands and wives and parents and children.

Ice-Breaker / 15 Minutes

Myself as an Appliance. Use this ice-breaker to start off this session on family relationships. Go around on question 1 and let everyone share. Then go around again on question 2.

1. If you could compare the role you have taken in your family down through time to a household appliance, what appliance would it be?
❐ vacuum cleaner—I pick up after everyone.
❐ heater—When people come in from the cold world I warm them up!
❐ television—I'm the entertainer.
❐ smoke alarm—I keep others alert to dangers.
❐ thermostat—I keep things comfortable.
❐ refrigerator—I provide all of the good stuff people seem to want.
❐ electric screwdriver—I fix things and keep them running.
❐ washing machine agitator—When things get too calm and boring I stir things up!

2. How happy are you with this role right now?

Bible Study / 30 Minutes

Option 1 / Gospel Study

Luke 15:11–32 / A Family Conflict

Read Luke 15:11–32 and discuss your responses to the following questions with your group. This is one of Jesus' most famous parables, and was told in response to the outrage of the Pharisees (the religious leaders of the time) over Jesus' association with people who were "sinners."

11Jesus continued: "There was a man who had two sons. 12The younger one said to his father, 'Father, give me my share of the estate.' So he divided his property between them.

13"Not long after that, the younger son got together all he had, set off for a distant country and there squandered his wealth in wild living. 14After he had spent everything, there was a severe famine in that whole country, and he began to be in need. 15So he went and hired himself out to a citizen of that country, who sent him to his fields to feed pigs. 16He longed to fill his stomach with the pods that the pigs were eating, but no one gave him anything.

[17]"When he came to his senses, he said, 'How many of my father's hired men have food to spare, and here I am starving to death! [18]I will set out and go back to my father and say to him: Father, I have sinned against heaven and against you. [19]I am no longer worthy to be called your son; make me like one of your hired men.' [20]So he got up and went to his father.

"But while he was still a long way off, his father saw him and was filled with compassion for him; he ran to his son, threw his arms around him and kissed him.

[21]"The son said to him, 'Father, I have sinned against heaven and against you. I am no longer worthy to be called your son.'

[22]"But the father said to his servants, 'Quick! Bring the best robe and put it on him. Put a ring on his finger and sandals on his feet. [23]Bring the fattened calf and kill it. Let's have a feast and celebrate. [24]For this son of mine was dead and is alive again; he was lost and is found.' So they began to celebrate.

[25]"Meanwhile, the older son was in the field. When he came near the house, he heard music and dancing. [26]So he called one of the servants and asked him what was going on. [27]'Your brother has come,' he replied, 'and your father has killed the fattened calf because he has him back safe and sound.'

[28]"The older brother became angry and refused to go in. So his father went out and pleaded with him. [29]But he answered his father, 'Look! All these years I've been slaving for you and never disobeyed your orders. Yet you never gave me even a young goat so I could celebrate with my friends. [30]But when this son of yours who has squandered your property with prostitutes comes home, you kill the fattened calf for him!'

[31]"'My son,' the father said, 'you are always with me, and everything I have is yours. [32]But we had to celebrate and be glad, because this brother of yours was dead and is alive again; he was lost and is found.' "

1. Which character do you identify with in this story? Why?
- ❏ the younger son—I've squandered my allowance (and even sown a few wild oats).
- ❏ the older son—I've resented younger siblings who got privileges I didn't.
- ❏ the waiting father—My kids keep me up at night.
- ❏ the narrator—I'm a spectator watching what God is doing.
- ❏ the younger son—I've experienced grace despite my actions.
- ❏ the older son—I've felt that I've had to be good.
- ❏ the pigs—I've been with prodigals who have hit bottom.

2. When did you leave home for the first time? What were some of the circumstances surrounding your departure? Where did you go when you left your parents' home? What were your feelings at that time?

3. If you were the father, what would have been your response when your son returned?
   ❑ "Good to see you—but you're grounded!"
   ❑ "You have disgraced the family."
   ❑ "I don't approve of what you've done, but you're still my son."
   ❑ "Welcome home, son—I love you."
   ❑ "Do you realize how much I have worried about you all this time?"

4. If you were the younger son, how would you feel when you first saw your father again?
   ❑ scared   ❑ grateful
   ❑ unworthy   ❑ guilty
   ❑ relieved   ❑ loved

5. If you had been the older brother, how would you have felt when you found out your father was throwing a party for your little brother?
   ❑ angry   ❑ happy
   ❑ confused   ❑ resentful
   ❑ let down

6. What in this story is most like your own story?
   ❑ Like the younger son, I had my time of rebellion.
   ❑ Like the older son, I've felt that I had to be good.
   ❑ Like the father, I have had to face the painful decision of whether or not to let a loved one go their own way.
   ❑ Like the wayward son, I have experienced grace.
   ❑ Like the older brother, I have felt cheated or left out.
   ❑ Like the younger brother, I have felt the jealousy of someone close to me.
   ❑ Like the father and younger son, I have experienced—the joy of reconciliation in a special relationship.
   ❑ other:_____

7. Which of the father's qualities do you most need?
   ❑ his willingness to let his son make mistakes
   ❑ his patience in waiting for change
   ❑ his understanding in dealing with both his children
   ❑ his ability to celebrate life

8. Which relationship in your family generates the most conflict? Why?
   ❑ father and son   ❑ father and daughter
   ❑ mother and son   ❑ mother and daughter
   ❑ brother and brother   ❑ sister and sister
   ❑ sister and brother   ❑ husband and wife
   ❑ myself and an in-law   ❑ other:_____

9. If you were to have a party to celebrate the most positive thing about your family, what would you celebrate? What healing change would need to happen in your family for you to be able to celebrate more fully?

10. Spiritually, in your relationship with God, where are you right now?
   ❏ never left home
   ❏ still at home, but itching to check out the "distant country"
   ❏ in the distant country, trying to have a good time
   ❏ starting to realize I'm in a pigpen
   ❏ nervously heading home to God, not knowing what to expect
   ❏ just beginning to feel God's forgiveness
   ❏ gradually feeling God's acceptance
   ❏ celebrating with the family of God
   ❏ other:_____

Option 2 / Epistle Study

Ephesians 5:21–6:4 / Family Relations

Read Ephesians 5:21–6:4, and discuss the questions which follow with your group. In this passage, Paul encourages Christians to treat each other lovingly in family relationships.

21 Submit to one another out of reverence for Christ.

22 Wives, submit to your husbands as to the Lord. 23 For the husband is the head of the wife as Christ is the head of the church, his body, of which he is the Savior. 24 Now as the church submits to Christ, so also wives should submit to their husbands in everything.

25 Husbands, love your wives, just as Christ loved the church and gave himself up for her 26 to make her holy, cleansing her by the washing with water through the word, 27 and to present her to himself as a radiant church, without stain or wrinkle or any other blemish, but holy and blameless. 28 In this same way, husbands ought to love their wives as their own bodies. He who loves his wife loves himself. 29 After all, no one ever hated his own body, but he feeds and cares for it, just as Christ does the church— 30 for we are members of his body. 31 "For this reason a man will leave his father and mother and be united to his wife, and the two will become one flesh." 32 This is a profound mystery—but I am talking about Christ and the church. 33 However, each one of you also must love his wife as he loves himself, and the wife must respect her husband.

6 *Children, obey your parents in the Lord, for this is right. 2 "Honor your father and mother"—which is the first commandment with a promise— 3 "that it may go well with you and that you may enjoy long life on the earth."*

4 Fathers, do not exasperate your children; instead, bring them up in the training and instruction of the Lord.

Leadership Training Supplement

YOU ARE
HERE

BIRTH	GROWTH	RELEASE

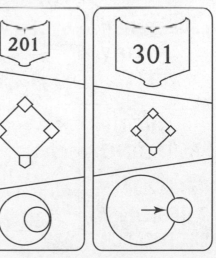

What is the game plan for your group in the 101 stage?

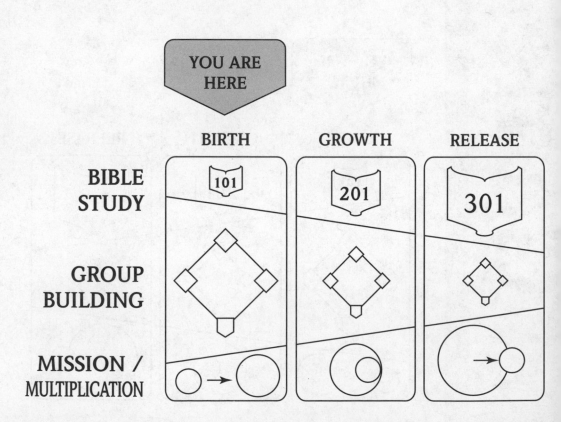

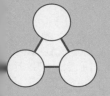

e 3-Legged Stool

The three essentials in a healthy small group are Bible Study, Group Building and Mission / Multiplication. You need all three to stay balanced—like a 3-legged stool.

- To focus only on Bible Study will lead to scholasticism.
- To focus only on Group Building will lead to narcissism.
- To focus only on Mission will lead to burnout.

You need a game plan for the life cycle of the group where all three of these elements are present in a mission-driven strategy. In the first stage of the group, here is the game plan:

Bible Study

To share your spiritual story through Scripture.

The greatest gift you can give a group is the gift of your spiritual story—the story of your spiritual beginnings, your spiritual growing pains, struggles, hopes and fears. The Bible Study is designed to help you tell your spiritual story to the group.

Group Building

To become a caring community.

In the first stage of a group, note how the baseball diamond is larger than the book and the circles. This is because Group Building is the priority in the first stage. Group Building is a four-step process to become a close-knit group. Using the baseball diamond illustration, the goal of Group Building—bonding—is home plate. But to get there you have to go around the bases.

Mission / Multiplication

To grow your group numerically and spiritually.

The mission of your group is the greatest mission anyone can give their life to—to bring new people into a personal relationship with Christ and the fellowship of a Christian community. This purpose will become more prominent in the second and third stages of your group. In this stage, the goal is to invite new people into your group and try to double.

M3

Bible Study

In the first stage of a group, the Bible Study is where you get to know each other and share your spiritual stories. The Bible Study is designed to give the leader the option of going LIGHT or HEAVY, depending on the background of the people in the group. OPTION 1 is especially designed for beginner groups who do not know a lot about the Bible or each other. OPTION 2 is for groups who are familiar with the Bible and with one another.

Option 1   Relational Bible Study (Stories)

Designed around a guided questionnaire, the questions move across the Disclosure Scale from "no risk" questions about people in the Bible story to "high risk" questions about your own life and how you would react in that situation. "If you had been in the story ..." or "The person in the story like me is ... " The questions are open-ended—with multiple-choice options and no right or wrong answers. A person with no background knowledge of the Bible may actually have the advantage because the questions are based on first impressions.

The STORY in Scripture	GUIDED QUESTIONNAIRE 1 2 3 4 5 6 7 8	My STORY compared

OPTION 1: Light RELATIONAL BIBLE STUDY	OPTION 2: Heavy INDUCTIVE BIBLE STUDY
• Based on Bible stories • Open-ended questions • To share your spiritual story	• Based on Bible teachings • With observation questions • To dig into Scripture

Option 2   Inductive Bible Study (Teachings)

For groups who know each other, OPTION 2 gives you the choice to go deeper in Bible Study, with questions about the text on three levels:

- Observation: What is the text saying?
- Interpretation: What does it mean?
- Application: What are you going to do about it?

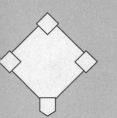

Group Building

The Baseball Diamond illustrates the four-step sharing process in bonding to become a group: (1) input; (2) feedback; (3) deeper input; and (4) deeper feedback. This process is carefully structured into the seven sessions of this course, as follows:

 Sharing My Story. My religious background. My early years and where I am right now in my spiritual journey.

 Affirming Each Other's Story. "Thank you for sharing ..." "Your story became a gift to me ..." "Your story helps me to understand where you are coming from ..."

 Sharing My Needs. "This is where I'm struggling and hurting. This is where I need to go—what I need to do."

 Caring for One Another. "How can we help you in prayer this week?" Ministry occurs as the group members serve one another through the Holy Spirit.

Mission / Multiplication

To prove that your group is "Mission-Driven," now is the time to start praying for your new "baby"—a new group to be born in the future. This is the MISSION of your group.

The birthing process begins by growing your group to about 10 or 12 people. Here are three suggestions to help your group stay focused on your Mission:

1. **Empty Chair.** Pull up an empty chair at the Caring Time and ask God to fill this chair at the next meeting.

2. **Refrigerator List.** Jot down the names of people you are going to invite and put this list on the refrigerator.

3. **New Member Home.** Move to the home of the newest member—where their friends will feel comfortable when they come to the group. On the next page, some of your questions about bringing new people into your group are answered.

What if a new person joins the group in the third or fourth session?

Call the "Option Play" and go back to an OPTION 1 Bible Study that allows this person to "share their story" and get to know the people in the group.

What do you do when the group gets too large for sharing?

Take advantage of the three-part agenda and subdivide into groups of four for the Bible Study time. Count off around the group: "one, two, one, two"—and have the "ones" move quickly to another room for sharing.

What is the long-term expectation of the group for mission?

To grow the size of the group and eventually start a new group after one or two years.

What do you do when the group does not want to multiply?

This is the reason why this MISSION needs to be discussed at the beginning of a group—not at the end. If the group is committed to this MISSION at the outset, and works on this mission in stage one, they will be ready for multiplication at the end of the final stage.

What are the principles behind the Serendipity approach to Bible Study for a beginner group?

1. *Level the Playing Field.* Start the sharing with things that are easy to talk about and where everyone is equal—things that are instantly recallable—light, mischievously revealing and childlike. Meet at the human side before moving into spiritual things.

2. *Share Your Spiritual Story.* Group Building, especially for new groups, is essential. It is crucial for Bible Study in beginner groups to help the group become a community by giving everyone the opportunity to share their spiritual history.

3. *Open Questions / Right Brain.* Open-ended questions are better than closed questions. Open questions allow for options, observations and a variety of opinions in which no one is right or wrong. Similarly, "right-brained" questions are

better than "left-brained" questions. Right-brained questions seek out your first impressions, tone, motives and subjective feelings about the text. Right-brained questions work well with narratives. Multiple-choice questionnaires encourage people who know very little about the Bible. Given a set of multiple-choice options, a new believer is not threatened, and a shy person is not intimidated. Everyone has something to contribute.

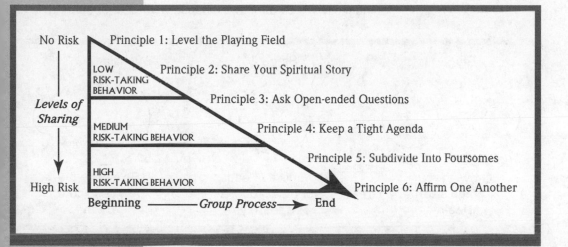

No Risk — Principle 1: Level the Playing Field

LOW RISK-TAKING BEHAVIOR — Principle 2: Share Your Spiritual Story

Levels of Sharing — Principle 3: Ask Open-ended Questions

MEDIUM RISK-TAKING BEHAVIOR — Principle 4: Keep a Tight Agenda

Principle 5: Subdivide Into Foursomes

HIGH RISK-TAKING BEHAVIOR

High Risk — Principle 6: Affirm One Another

Beginning ——— *Group Process* ➔ End

4. *Tight Agenda.* A tight agenda is better than a loose agenda for beginning small groups. Those people who might be nervous about "sharing" will find comfort knowing that the meeting agenda has been carefully organized. The more structure the first few meetings have the better, especially for a new group. Some people are afraid that a structured agenda will limit discussion. In fact, the opposite is true. The Serendipity agenda is designed to keep the discussion focused on what's important and to bring out genuine feelings, issues, and areas of need. If the goal is to move the group toward deeper relationships and a deeper experience of God, then a structured agenda is the best way to achieve that goal.

5. *Fearless Foursomes.* Dividing your small group into foursomes during the Bible Study can be a good idea. In groups of four, everyone will have an opportunity to participate and you can finish the Bible Study in 30 minutes. In groups of eight or more, the Bible Study will need to be longer and you will take away from the Caring Time.

Also, by subdividing into groups of four for the Bible Study time, you give others a chance to develop their skills at leading a group—in preparation for the day when you develop a small cell to eventually move out and birth a new group.

6. *Affirm the person and their story.* Give positive feedback to group members: "Thank you for sharing ... " "Your story really helps me to understand where you are coming from ... " "Your story was a real gift to me ... " This affirmation given honestly will create the atmosphere for deeper sharing.

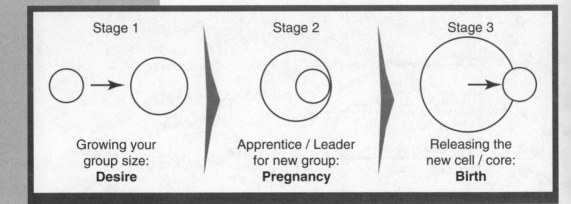

Stage 1	Stage 2	Stage 3
Growing your group size: **Desire**	Apprentice / Leader for new group: **Pregnancy**	Releasing the new cell / core: **Birth**

What is the next stage of our group all about?

In the next stage, the 201 BIBLE STUDY is deeper, GROUP BUILDING focuses on developing your gifts, and in the MISSION you will identify an Apprentice / Leader and two others within your group who will eventually become the leadership core of a new group down the road a bit.

1. How would you describe your parents' relationship when you were growing up? How would you describe your relationship with your parents when you were growing up?

2. What couple do you know who has a really good marriage? What makes it work?

3. What does it mean for wives to "submit to your husbands as to the Lord" (see note, "submit," on 5:22)? What does it mean for husbands to "love your wives, just as Christ loved the church"?

4. Does society's emphasis on equality in marriage conflict with these verses? If so, how? If not, why not?

5. What does God ask of children (6:1–2)? In what practical ways can we "honor" our parents?

6. What does God ask of parents (6:4)? What does it mean to you to bring up children "in the training and instruction of the Lord"?

7. What is the difference between "exasperating" children and practicing "tough love"? What are your feelings about the discipline you received from your parents? If you are a parent, what are your feelings about the discipline your children have received from you?

8. What qualities would characterize a home where the members of the family applied the principles of this Scripture passage consistently? How close is that to your family now? What is the message of this Scripture for your family situation?

9. If you were to love the people in your family "as Christ loves the church," how would it change your family? What is one way you can go about doing this in the coming week?

Caring Time / 15–45 Minutes

Take time at the close to share any personal prayer requests and answer the question:

"How can we help you in prayer this week?"

Close with a short time of prayer, remembering the concerns and struggles voiced during this meeting. If you would like to pray in silence, say the word "Amen" when you finish your prayer, so that the next person will know when to start.

Summary. Paul turns to the need for quality relationships at home and at work. He comments on three crucial relationships: that between husband and wife (5:22–33); that between parent and child (6:1–4); and that between master and slave (6:5–9). These three sets of relationships—within marriage, across generations, and in the workplace—form the core of most people's lives, and it is crucial that they be lived in accord with the will of Christ if a Christian is to be all he or she can be.

5:22 The verb in verse 21 ("submit") is linked grammatically both backward to 5:18 and forward to this verse. Looking backward, "submit" is the last of four present participles which describe what is involved in being filled with the Spirit. Looking forward, "submit" provides the verb for this verse which has no verb of its own.

Wives. In a radical departure from tradition, Paul addresses women in their own right as individuals, able to make their own choices. He does not address them through their husbands (as would have been common in the first century). He does not tell husbands: "Make your wives submit to you."

submit. This injunction from Paul must be understood in its historical context. In Jewish law, a woman was a "thing," not a person, and she had no legal rights. In describing the Greek world, Demosthenes wrote: "We have courtesans for our pleasure, prostitutes for daily physical use, wives to bring up legitimate children." In Rome, too, divorce was easy, and women were repressed. Against this, Paul proposes a radical, liberating view: (1) submission was to be mutual (the man was no longer the absolute authority); (2) wives are called upon to defer only to their husbands (and not to every man); and (3) submission is defined and qualified by Christ's headship of the church (Christ died for the church). Therefore, what wives are called to submit to ("yield to," "adapt to," or "give way to") is sacrificial love! Love, not control, is the issue.

to your husbands. A woman owes submission only to her husband, not to all men (as first-century culture taught).

5:23 *Christ is the head of the church.* It is a headship of love, not of control; of nurture, not of suppression. Had Paul wanted to convey the idea that the husband "rules over" the wife (as Christ "rules over" the church), he would have used a different Greek word for "head."

the Savior. The emphasis in this analogy is not on Christ as Lord, but on Christ as Savior. Paul is not saying that husbands are to express "headship" via the exertion of some sort of authority (as befits a "lord"), but via the expression of sacrificial love (as characterized by the Savior).

5:25–33 Having addressed the role of wives in three verses, Paul now devotes nine verses to explain to men what mutual submission means for them! Nowhere in these verses does Paul define the husband's role in terms of authority over his wife. In fact, the word "authority" (*exousia*) is not used once in 5:22–6:9.

5:25 *love your wives.* This is the main thing Paul says to husbands. It is so important that he repeats this injunction three times (vv. 25,28,33). Love is what the husband gives by way of his part in the mutual submission paradigm. This attitude stands in contrast to Jewish teaching. "The rabbis asserted that money, the contract, and intercourse make marriage. When they enumerated what else a man 'owed' to his wife, they seldom mentioned love" (Barth). As for Greek culture, although certain philosophers such as Aristotle taught that men ought to love their wives, they used a mild word for love (*phileo*) signifying the sort of affection a person has for family. Here, however, Paul urges a far stronger type of love: *agape,* which is characterized by sacrificial, self-giving action.

just as Christ loved the church and gave himself up for her. Paul now makes quite clear in what sense he is speaking of Christ as head over the church. Two actions characterize Christ's role for the church: love and sacrifice. The husband is called upon to act toward his wife in the same way— that is, to die for her! (This is how Christ "gave himself up for the church.")

5:25–27 In comparing the marriage relationship to the relationship between Christ and the church, Paul is following a long tradition in Scripture. The Old Testament often pictured God's relationship to his people in terms of a marriage covenant (Isa. 54:4–6; Jer. 2:1–3; 31:31–32; Hos. 1:3). In the New Testament, Christ is seen as the bridegroom (Mark 2:19–20; John 3:29).

5:28–31 In describing how husbands are to love their wives, Paul turns from the rather exalted vision of Christ's love for the church to the more mundane (but entirely realistic) level of the husband's love for himself!

5:31 *one flesh.* Paul does not view marriage as some sort of spiritual covenant devoid of sexuality. His second illustration of how a husband is to love his wife (vv. 28–31) revolves around their sexual union, as is made explicit here by his quotation of Genesis 2:24.

5:33 *as he loves himself.* The gauge by which husbands will know if they are, indeed, loving their wives properly is self-love: "Is this how I want to be loved?" (see also Lev. 19:18).

respect. This means to honor and build up another person.

6:1–3 Paul does not simply command obedience on the part of children. He gives reasons for it. In other words, Paul does not take obedience for granted. In the same way that he addressed husbands and wives (and gave each a rationale for their behavior), he also does the same for children.

6:1 *Children.* The very fact that Paul even addresses children is remarkable. Normally, all such instructions would come via their parents. That he addresses children in this public letter means that children were in attendance with their families at worship when such a letter would have been read. Paul does not define a "child" here; i.e., he does not deal with the question of when a child becomes an adult, and thus ceases to be under parental authority. This is not a real problem, however, since each culture has its own definition of when adulthood begins. Even as adults, though, children are expected to "honor" their parents.

obey. Paul tells the children to "obey" ("follow," "be subject to," literally, "listen to"). He uses a different word from the one used when speaking of the relationship between wives and husbands. Parents have authority over their children, but not husbands over wives. Also, although "obey" is a stronger word than "submit," it is not without limits.

in the Lord. This is the first reason children are to obey their parents. There are two ways in which this phrase can be taken: Obey your parents because you are a Christian, and/or obey your parents in everything that is compatible with your commitment to Christ.

for this is right. This is the second of four reasons Paul gives for obedience.

6:2 *"Honor your father and mother."* Paul begins to quote the fifth commandment. This is the third reason children should obey parents. God commands it. "To honor father and mother means more than to obey them, especially if this obedience is interpreted in a merely outward sense. It is the inner attitude of the child toward his parents that comes to the fore in the requirement that he honor them. All selfish obedience or reluctant obedience, or obedience under terror is immediately ruled out. To honor implies to love, to regard highly, to show the spirit of respect and consideration" (Hendriksen).

6:3 This is the fourth reason for obedience. It produces good rewards. Paul identifies the two aspects of the promise: material well-being and long life. The promise is probably not for individual children, but for the community of which they are a part. It will be prosperous and long-standing.

6:4 Just as children have a duty to obey, parents have the duty to instruct children with gentleness and restraint.

Fathers. The model for a father is that of God, the "Father of all" (4:6). This view of fatherhood stands in sharp contrast to the harsh Roman father, who had the power of life and death over his children.

exasperate. Parents are to be responsible for not provoking hostility on the part of their children. By humiliating children, being cruel to them, overindulging them, or being unreasonable, parents squash children (rather than encourage them).

SESSION
5

Loving Christians

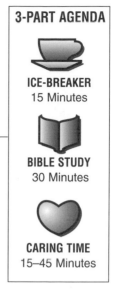

3-PART AGENDA

ICE-BREAKER
15 Minutes

BIBLE STUDY
30 Minutes

CARING TIME
15–45 Minutes

Being a member of the Christian family is similar to membership in any family. There is a strong common bond which unites us. But that doesn't mean that we will always agree with other family members (or that we will always get along). What is our responsibility to fellow believers? Two of our major responsibilities are having an attitude of servanthood and working toward unity.

Many Christians are moving away from a perspective of self-fulfillment to a desire to give themselves to something beyond themselves—to serve others. Albert Schweitzer said repeatedly that as long as there was a person in the world who was hungry, sick, lonely or living in fear, that person was his responsibility. He affirmed this by living a life based on this belief—a life of servanthood. We grow as we help others. As we meet their needs, we discover the ability to share our own needs and they, too, can be met. This is part of a fulfilling life.

Besides having the attitude of a servant, we must also work toward unity. How do we get along with fellow believers when we do not agree with them on a theological or moral issue? It has been said that the most divisive group of people can be found within the walls of a church. What is our responsibility to others within our community of faith?

> **LEADER: If you haven't already, now is the time to start thinking about the next step for your group. Take a look at the 201 courses (the second stage in the small group life cycle) on the inside of the back cover.**

In Option 1 (from John's Gospel), we will consider the example Jesus gave his disciples when he washed their feet. In our Option 2 Study (from 1 Corinthians), we will consider Paul's exhortation concerning unity which he wrote to the church at Corinth.

Ice-Breaker / 15 Minutes

Music in My Life. Taking one category at a time, put an *"X"* on the line to indicate how you are feeling right now. Go around the group and share your answers.

MY DAY TODAY HAS BEEN ...
Will Tomorrow Never Come? _____ Zippity Doo-dah!
(My oh my what a wonderful day!)

IN MY WORK THIS PAST WEEK ...
The Thrill Is Gone _____ I've Got a Good Thing Going

IN MY FAMILY LIFE, I'M FEELING LIKE ...
Stormy Weather _____ The Sound of Music

ABOUT THE FUTURE, I'M FEELING ...
All Shook Up _____ Don't Worry, Be Happy

IN MY SPIRITUAL LIFE, I'M FEELING LIKE ...
Sounds of Silence _____ Hallelujah Chorus

Bible Study / 30 Minutes

Option 1 / Gospel Study

John 13:1–17 / A Life of Service

The following passage describes an event during the Last Supper (which Jesus celebrated with his disciples) on the night before his death. It was customary for people's dusty, sandaled feet to be washed, usually by the lowest-ranking servant, before a meal was served. Read John 13:1–17 and discuss the questions which follow with your group.

13 *It was just before the Passover Feast. Jesus knew that the time had come for him to leave this world and go to the Father. Having loved his own who were in the world, he now showed them the full extent of his love.*

²The evening meal was being served, and the devil had already prompted Judas Iscariot, son of Simon, to betray Jesus. ³Jesus knew that the Father had put all things under his power, and that he had come from God and was returning to God; *so he got up from the meal, took off his outer clothing, and wrapped a towel around his waist. *After that, he poured water into a basin and began to wash his disciples' feet, drying them with the towel that was wrapped around him.

*He came to Simon Peter, who said to him, "Lord, are you going to wash my feet?"

*Jesus replied, "You do not realize now what I am doing, but later you will understand."

*"No," said Peter, "you shall never wash my feet."

Jesus answered, "Unless I wash you, you have no part with me."

*"Then, Lord," Simon Peter replied, "not just my feet but my hands and my head as well!"

*Jesus answered, "A person who has had a bath needs only to wash his feet; his whole body is clean. And you are clean, though not every one of you." *For he knew who was going to betray him, and that was why he said not every one was clean.

*When he had finished washing their feet, he put on his clothes and returned to his place. "Do you understand what I have done for you?" he asked them. *"You call me 'Teacher' and 'Lord,' and rightly so, for that is what I am. *Now that I, your Lord and Teacher, have washed your feet, you also should wash one another's feet. *I have set you an example that you should do as I have done for you. *I tell you the truth, no servant is greater than his master, nor is a messenger greater than the one who sent him. *Now that you know these things, you will be blessed if you do them."

1. What is your first impression of this story about footwashing?
   ❒ This is confusing.   ❒ This is moving.
   ❒ This is embarrassing.   ❒ This is gross.
   ❒ This is irrelevant for our culture.
   ❒ This is a model for any culture.

2. What would you have done if you had been there and Jesus started to wash your feet?
   ❒ left the room   ❒ refused to let him
   ❒ broken down and cried   ❒ felt honored by his caring act
   ❒ just sat there—feeling guilty and unworthy
   ❒ jumped up and tried to wash *his* feet

3. When Jesus told his disciples that they should wash one another's feet, he meant:
   ❒ Their feet were so dirty they needed a second wash.
   ❒ Footwashing should be observed regularly, like Communion.
   ❒ They should be willing to do the lowliest tasks in service to others.
   ❒ No one should do all the servant-tasks—they should share them.

4. Who is one person in your life who has demonstrated what it means to "wash feet"? What did that person do for you?

"Jesus deliberately turned his back on all the ideas of power held in the world and proposed something new: servanthood."
—Arthur M. Adams

5. When you were in the seventh grade, what kind of servant-tasks were you expected to do around the house?

❐ make my bed   ❐ look after my sibling(s)
❐ clean my room   ❐ do yard work
❐ take out the trash   ❐ help with cooking
❐ wash the dishes   ❐ all of the above
❐ dust and vacuum   ❐ none of the above
❐ do laundry

6. How did you feel about doing those tasks? What ingenious ways did you come up with to avoid them?

7. What do you do for others right now which is most like "washing feet"—a somewhat unpleasant, humble servant-task? How do you feel about doing this?

8. Which of the following is true in relationship to your church involvement and servanthood?

❐ My church involvement has nothing to do with serving—it's about showing up on Sunday morning.
❐ My church involvement requires many servant-tasks, but most of them are pleasant.
❐ My church involvement requires many servant-tasks, most of which are not pleasant.
❐ The main pleasure I get from church comes from serving people.
❐ I chose my church specifically so I wouldn't have to do unpleasant tasks like that.

9. What would it mean for you to take on the servant-mind of Christ, particularly in relation to your church involvement?

❐ Sounds like I would have to choose something unpleasant.
❐ I would have to change my attitude.
❐ I would focus more on the needs of people than on showing up.
❐ I would need to be willing to do things that aren't "my job."
❐ I would have to realize that self-fulfillment can only come if I am committed to serving others.
❐ I would have to do a lot of things I'm not willing to do right now.
❐ I am trying to have this attitude.
❐ other:_____

Option 2 / Epistle Study

LEADER: If you are using the Option 2 Study for this session, you may want to see the "Comment" on the topic of unity on pages 42–43.

1 Corinthians 12:12–27 / Body Support

One of the main reasons Paul wrote 1 Corinthians was to challenge the church at Corinth to live in unity. Though there are as many "parts" as there are believers, there is only one "body"—the body of Christ. Read 1 Corinthians 12:12–27 and discuss the questions that follow.

¹²The body is a unit, though it is made up of many parts; and though all its parts are many, they form one body. So it is with Christ. ¹³For we were all baptized by one Spirit into one body—whether Jews or Greeks, slave or free—and we were all given the one Spirit to drink.

¹⁴Now the body is not made up of one part but of many. ¹⁵If the foot should say, "Because I am not a hand, I do not belong to the body," it would not for that reason cease to be part of the body. ¹⁶And if the ear should say, "Because I am not an eye, I do not belong to the body," it would not for that reason cease to be part of the body. ¹⁷If the whole body were an eye, where would the sense of hearing be? If the whole body were an ear, where would the sense of smell be? ¹⁸But in fact God has arranged the parts in the body, every one of them, just as he wanted them to be. ¹⁹If they were all one part, where would the body be? ²⁰As it is, there are many parts, but one body.

²¹The eye cannot say to the hand, "I don't need you!" And the head cannot say to the feet, "I don't need you!" ²²On the contrary, those parts of the body that seem to be weaker are indispensable, ²³and the parts that we think are less honorable we treat with special honor. And the parts that are unpresentable are treated with special modesty, ²⁴while our presentable parts need no special treatment. But God has combined the members of the body and has given greater honor to the parts that lacked it, ²⁵so that there should be no division in the body, but that its parts should have equal concern for each other. ²⁶If one part suffers, every part suffers with it; if one part is honored, every part rejoices with it.

²⁷Now you are the body of Christ, and each one of you is a part of it.

1. What is one talent you have that the others in this group may not know about?

2. When have you felt like you were part of a close-knit unit, where everyone really accepted each other (a sports team, a music group, a military unit, a sorority, a church group, etc.)?

3. In what ways do verses 12–13 illustrate the unity of believers?

4. In verses 14–21, do the foot and the ear have an inferiority complex or a superiority complex?

5. How could you illustrate the truth of verse 26 from your own body? From your church?

6. Which parts of the body do you identify with the most?
   ❏ a foot—I'll go anywhere to serve God.
   ❏ a hand—I like to help out.
   ❏ an ear—I'm a good listener.
   ❏ an eye—I can see what needs to be done.
   ❏ a leg—I keep things moving.
   ❏ the head—I'm fulfilled by leading or organizing.
   ❏ the mouth—I express myself well.
   ❏ other:_____

7. How does this passage make you feel about your place in the body of Christ? About your need for others?

8. How connected are you to your church body? How can you help the "body" function better?

COMMENT

The quality of fellowship in the early church was both striking and appealing—striking because it contrasted so sharply with what occurred in other institutions, and appealing because its very quality made men and women hungry to be a part of it. At the heart of this new fellowship was the eradication of those barriers that had divided the ancient world: race, class, and gender. "There is neither Jew nor Greek, slave nor free, male nor female, for you are all one in Christ Jesus" is how Paul expresses this truth in Galatians 3:28.

This kind of tradition-breaking unity was first modeled by our Lord in his selection of the 12 disciples. He included in his band a pair of traditional enemies: Simon the naturalistic Jewish zealot who was a member of an anti-Roman, guerrilla-like group and Matthew who worked for the Roman government collecting their hated taxes. The contrast in temperaments is sharp also. Peter, James and John were aggressive and often blunt while some disciples were so low-key that you hear of them only when the list of 12 names is given. (What was the role of the apostle Thaddaeus?)

This same unexpected unity is seen in the early church. For example, in the church in Antioch we find the aristocrat Manaen ("who had been brought up with Herod the tetrarch"); the rigid and fire-filled ex-Pharisee Paul; Barnabas the encourager who was a landowner in Cyprus and a member of the tribe from which temple officials were drawn; Lucian, a

Hellenistic Jew from Cyrene and Simeon "the Swarthy" who was most probably a black African. They were gathered together to worship, fast and pray (Acts 13:1–3).

What created this unity? At its core, of course, was the transforming death and resurrection of Jesus Christ which drew people together into new relationships. This fellowship was then deepened as Christians "devoted themselves to the apostles' teaching and to the fellowship, to the breaking of bread and to prayer" (Acts 2:42). The unity was maintained because problems and aberrations were not allowed to disrupt the fellowship. In Galatians 2:11–21 and elsewhere, Paul, as well as the other apostles, deals swiftly and directly with such problems lest they take root and destroy this new unity. (Adapted from *Evangelism in the Early Church* by Michael Green [Eerdmans], pp. 180–183.)

What has happened to our unity? Denominations now number in the hundreds. Even though many groups confess a common faith in the Lord Jesus Christ, denominational lines and religious labels are drawn tightly. Ask 50 people from the street if they are Christians. Chances are good that they would not identify themselves as Christians or non-Christians, but as Methodists or Presbyterians or Catholics or Baptists. So much for our unity. The unity Christ desires is one that strengthens and encourages us on our pilgrimage. In fact, when that type of unity is present, we begin to walk in such confidence that there's a definite hint of invincibility in our faith.

Caring Time / 15–45 Minutes

Take time at the close to share any personal prayer requests. Answer the question:

LEADER: Ask the group, "Who are you going to invite next week?"

"How can we help you in prayer this week?"

Then go around and let each person pray for the person on their right. Finish the sentence,

"Dear God, I want to speak to you about my friend _____."

As you close, include a prayer for the bonding of your group members, as well as for the numerical growth of the group.

Reference Notes

Summary. Having pointed out the diversity of gifts in 12:1–11 (thus drawing the Corinthians away from their preoccupation with one gift—tongues), now Paul examines the unity that exists within all this diversity. Once having established that Christians are all part of one body (vv. 12–13), Paul returns then to the idea of diversity, in which he not only points out the variety of gifts that exist, but the fact that none are inferior and all are necessary.

12:12 *a unit ... made up of many parts.* This is Paul's central point in verses 12–30: "diversity within unity" (Fee).

So it is with Christ. The church is the body of Christ (v. 27), and so indeed Christ can be understood to be made up of many parts. Yet he is also the Lord (12:3), and thus head over that church.

12:13 Here Paul points to the unity side of the body of Christ. Unity exists because all were baptized into one Spirit, and all drink from one Spirit. His concern is not with how people become believers, but with how believers become one body. The term "baptism" is probably metaphorical (Fee). The way believers are "put into one Spirit" is like baptism; i.e., "think of it as being immersed in the Spirit."

baptized by one Spirit. In fact, the NIV footnoted translation of the preposition is probably the correct rendering: "baptized *in* one Spirit," since Paul's concern is not with the means by which believers are baptized, but with the common reality in which all believers exist; i.e., the Holy Spirit (Fee).

Jews or Greeks, slave or free. See Galatians 3:28.

one Spirit to drink. Paul continues speaking metaphorically, with the idea of water still dominant. Being incorporated into one body is not only like baptism, it is also like "drinking the same Spirit."

12:14 Now Paul points to the diversity side of the body of Christ (which is his major concern): the one body has many different parts to it—which his analogy will demonstrate.

12:15–26 Having established that all Christians are part of one body (which is, in fact, Christ's body) and that this body has a variety of parts, Paul then develops an elaborate metaphor based on the human body. He makes two points: There are a variety of gifts (vv. 15–20), and each gift is vital, regardless of its nature (vv. 21–26).

12:15–20 It is just as ludicrous for Christians to opt out of the body of Christ (presumably by not using their gifts during worship) because they have one gift and not another (presumably more desired) gift, as it is for a foot (or ear) to decide not to be a part of a physical body because it is not a hand (or eye).

12:17 If all Christians had the same gift, the body would be impoverished.

12:21–26 Just as it is presumptuous of the eye (or head) to say to the hand (or feet) that it has no need of it, so too, a Christian ought not to deny the value, need or function of anyone's spiritual gift, especially on the basis that it is different from (or inferior to) one's own gift.

12:21 Each part of the body needs the other parts. No one gift (e.g., tongues) can stand alone. Wholeness in the body requires that all the parts function together.

12:22 *weaker.* "The delicate organs, such as the eye; and the invisible organs such as the heart" (Barrett).

12:26 In fact, the whole person suffers when one (to use a modern example) sprains an ankle. It is not just the ankle that suffers.

12:27 Paul sums up the meaning of his metaphor.

the body of Christ. By this phrase, Paul conveys the idea not that Christ consists of this body, but that Christ rules over this body, and that this body belongs to him.

SESSION

6

Loving Non-Christians

3-PART AGENDA

ICE-BREAKER
15 Minutes

BIBLE STUDY
30 Minutes

CARING TIME
15–45 Minutes

In our previous session, we discussed the ways to strengthen our relationships with fellow believers. We discovered that through servanthood and pursuing unity (despite our diversity), our relationships can be made stronger. But what do we do with people who are outside the community of faith? We are not talking about those who hold a different view of a fine theological point, or even those who disagree with us politically. We are now looking at people who are not believers. We are talking about people we would not normally associate with. We may not associate with them because we grew up believing that we shouldn't associate with them. Depending on the area of the country we live in, these may be people who might even be Christians, but of a different faith.

The point is Jesus went out of his way to associate with people that the rest of society had considered to be outcasts. They may have been outcasts due to their low social standing, or because they had a particular disease or illness, or maybe because they were from a different country. Often we don't associate with certain type of people because of our

> **LEADER: This is the next to last session in this course. At the end of the course, how would you like to celebrate your time together? With a dinner? With a party? With a commitment to continue as a group?**

prejudices and stereotyping (and not because we have personally met them and didn't get along with them).

God's Word speaks about relating to and loving people outside the community of faith, and we will look at some of that Scripture in this session. In Option 1 (from John's Gospel), we will consider Jesus' example of breaking down cultural barriers. In Option 2 (from Paul's letter to the Romans), we will consider Paul's teaching about loving those outside of our faith.

To get started, take a few minutes to think about the things that drive you crazy by doing the following ice-breaker.

Ice-Breaker / 15 Minutes

Things That Drive You Crazy. Here's a list of things that drive a lot of people crazy. Do they drive you crazy, too? Take turns reading the different lines (person #1 reads line 1, person #2, line 2, and so on). Let others guess your answer before sharing your response.

	YES	NO	SOMETIMES
slow driver in the fast lane	❐	❐	❐
bathtub rings that aren't yours	❐	❐	❐
song that gets stuck in your head	❐	❐	❐
dripping faucet	❐	❐	❐
someone talking during a movie	❐	❐	❐
radio blaring in public	❐	❐	❐
losing one sock	❐	❐	❐
not enough toilet paper	❐	❐	❐
friend who is always late	❐	❐	❐
toilet seat left up	❐	❐	❐
toothpaste squeezed in the middle	❐	❐	❐
preempting of television program	❐	❐	❐
an itch you can't reach	❐	❐	❐
screeching chalk on blackboard	❐	❐	❐
pen that will not work	❐	❐	❐
people that crack their gum	❐	❐	❐
backseat driver	❐	❐	❐

Bible Study / 30 Minutes

Option 1 / Gospel Study

John 4:4–26 / Breaking Barriers

Instead of avoiding Samaria as Jews often did, Jesus crossed the boundary into this area that Jews considered inhabited by spiritual and ethnic half-breeds. The fact that Jesus made conversation with a woman—of irreputable character no less—was also amazing in that day and age. Read John 4:4–26 and discuss your responses to the following questions with the group.

4Now he had to go through Samaria. 5So he came to a town in Samaria called Sychar, near the plot of ground Jacob had given to his son Joseph. 6Jacob's well was there, and Jesus, tired as he was from the journey, sat down by the well. It was about the sixth hour.

7When a Samaritan woman came to draw water, Jesus said to her, "Will you give me a drink?" 8(His disciples had gone into the town to buy food.)

9The Samaritan woman said to him, "You are a Jew and I am a Samaritan woman. How can you ask me for a drink?" (For Jews do not associate with Samaritans.)

10Jesus answered her, "If you knew the gift of God and who it is that asks you for a drink, you would have asked him and he would have given you living water."

11"Sir," the woman said, "you have nothing to draw with and the well is deep. Where can you get this living water? 12Are you greater than our father Jacob, who gave us the well and drank from it himself, as did also his sons and his flocks and herds?"

13Jesus answered, "Everyone who drinks this water will be thirsty again, 14but whoever drinks the water I give him will never thirst. Indeed, the water I give him will become in him a spring of water welling up to eternal life."

15The woman said to him, "Sir, give me this water so that I won't get thirsty and have to keep coming here to draw water."

16He told her, "Go, call your husband and come back."

17"I have no husband," she replied.

Jesus said to her, "You are right when you say you have no husband. 18The fact is, you have had five husbands, and the man you now have is not your husband. What you have just said is quite true."

19"Sir," the woman said, "I can see that you are a prophet. 20Our fathers worshiped on this mountain, but you Jews claim that the place where we must worship is in Jerusalem."

21Jesus declared, "Believe me, woman, a time is coming when you will worship the Father neither on this mountain nor in Jerusalem. 22You Samaritans worship what you do not know; we worship what we do know, for salvation is from the Jews. 23Yet a time is coming and has now come when the true worshipers will worship the Father in spirit and truth, for they are the kind of worshipers the Father seeks. 24God is spirit, and his worshipers must worship in spirit and in truth."

25The woman said, "I know that Messiah" (called Christ) "is coming. When he comes, he will explain everything to us."

26Then Jesus declared, "I who speak to you am he."

1. How would you describe this woman's response for most of her conversation with Jesus?

❐ Puzzled—"Why would this Jewish man even talk to me?"

❐ Searching—"Is it possible this is what I've been looking for?"

❐ Avoidance—"I think I'd better try to change the subject."

❐ Skeptical—"Who does this guy think he is?!"

2. As someone who was taught from birth to despise Samaritans, how would you—as one of the disciples—feel when Jesus decided to go through Samaria instead of taking the long way home?

❒ I would have insisted that we take the longer route.

❒ I would have been upset at Jesus for going against our Jewish upbringing.

❒ I would have been afraid.

❒ I would have been excited about challenging the status quo.

❒ I would have been looking over my shoulder the whole time.

3. "Nice girls" didn't come to the well at noontime ("the sixth hour"). Why did Jesus risk his reputation to ask a favor of this woman?

❒ He wanted to challenge the status quo.

❒ It was an innocent request—he was simply thirsty.

❒ He wanted to see what she would do.

❒ Reputation didn't matter as much to him as loving people who were in need.

❒ He wanted to show that God sent him for everyone.

❒ other:_____

4. Jews did not associate with Samaritans. When you were growing up, what kind of people were you warned not to associate with?

❒ people of a different race   ❒ kids who used foul language

❒ foreigners   ❒ people of another religion

❒ people from "the other side of the tracks"

❒ people of a different political persuasion

❒ We could associate with anyone.

5. What does this story say to you about breaking down the barriers that exist between races, cultures, and other groups?

❒ It starts with talking and listening.

❒ It starts with not worrying about what others tell you about people, and learning for yourself.

❒ It comes from realizing we all "thirst" for the same things in life.

❒ It will happen when we follow Christ's example.

❒ other:_____

6. What do you need to help you overcome barriers in your "world"?

❒ I need a willingness to listen and learn.

❒ I need a willingness to see past differences.

❒ I need courage to reach out past the barriers.

❒ I need to look at others through God's eyes.

❒ I need to love others with God's love.

❒ other:_____

7. Jesus offered this woman "living water" for what she was thirsting for in life. What do you think she really wanted?
❏ intimacy in her relationships
❏ intimacy with God
❏ acceptance of who she was
❏ forgiveness for the life she had led
❏ meaning and purpose in life
❏ basic survival in life
❏ other:_____

8. What are you thirsting for most in life right now?
❏ close friendships
❏ closeness with God
❏ acceptance of who I am
❏ forgiveness
❏ meaning and purpose in life
❏ basic survival in life
❏ other:_____

9. What do you need to do to relieve your spiritual thirst?
❏ accept the forgiveness that Jesus offers
❏ enter into a real relationship with Christ
❏ seek Jesus' direction in my life
❏ reach out to people like Jesus did, especially past barriers
❏ practice more spiritual discipline—in private Bible study and prayer
❏ other:_____

Option 2 / Epistle Study

Romans 12:9–21 / Loving Outsiders

In this section of Paul's letter to the Romans, he describes relationships between Christians. Then he concludes this section by discussing (in verses 14–21) the question of how to relate to those who aren't Christians. Read Romans 12:9–21 and discuss your responses to the following questions with your group.

⁹Love must be sincere. Hate what is evil; cling to what is good. ¹⁰Be devoted to one another in brotherly love. Honor one another above yourselves. ¹¹Never be lacking in zeal, but keep your spiritual fervor, serving the Lord. ¹²Be joyful in hope, patient in affliction, faithful in prayer. ¹³Share with God's people who are in need. Practice hospitality.

¹⁴Bless those who persecute you; bless and do not curse. ¹⁵Rejoice with those who rejoice; mourn with those who mourn. ¹⁶Live in harmony with one another. Do not be proud, but be willing to associate with people of low position. Do not be conceited.

¹⁷Do not repay anyone evil for evil. Be careful to do what is right in the eyes of everybody. ¹⁸If it is possible, as far as it depends on you, live at peace with everyone. ¹⁹Do not take revenge, my friends, but leave room for God's wrath, for it is written: "It is mine to avenge; I will repay," says the Lord. ²⁰On the contrary:

> "If your enemy is hungry, feed him;
>   if he is thirsty, give him something to drink.
> In doing this, you will heap burning coals on his head."

²¹Do not be overcome by evil, but overcome evil with good.

1. What is the closest you've come to being persecuted for your faith?

"Man has no choice but to love. For when he does not, he finds his alternatives lie in loneliness, destruction and despair."
—Leo Buscaglia

2. When you feel you have been wronged, what do you generally do?
   ☐ "Grin and bear it.   ☐ "Forgive and forget."
   ☐ "I don't get mad; I get even."   ☐ other:_____

3. Which of the commands listed in these verses are easiest for you to keep? Which are hardest for you to keep?

4. In the first part of this passage (verses 9–13), how does love operate within the family of faith?

5. In the second part of this passage (vv. 14–21), how does love respond to those who are outside—maybe even hostile toward—the family of faith?

6. What effect on nonbelievers would the attitudes in this passage have (see, for instance, the note on v. 20)?

7. When is it harder for you to practice love—when you're hurt by someone close to you? Or when you're violated by someone outside your circle of family and friends? Why?

8. What can you do this week, in a practical way, to "live at peace" with someone who irritates you?

9. This past week have you felt more "overcome with evil" or have you "overcome evil with good"?

♥ Caring Time / 15–45 Minutes

Take time at the close to share any personal prayer requests. Answer the question:

"How can we help you in prayer this week?"

Then go around and let each person pray for the person on their right. Finish the sentence:

"Dear God, I want to speak to you about my friend _____."

Reference Notes

Summary. Paul now offers a series of loosely-connected exhortations by way of further explanation of Romans 12:1–2, focused first on relationships between Christians (vv. 9–13) and then on relationships with those outside the church (vv. 14–21).

12:9 *Love.* *Agape*, self-giving action on behalf of others made possible by God's Spirit. Thus far in Romans when Paul spoke of love, it was in reference to God's love. There is one exception to this, namely 8:28, where he speaks of a person's love for God. But here in 12:9 the focus shifts. Paul's concern is how the Christian relates to other people. This becomes especially clear in 13:8–10. "God in his love has claimed us wholly for Himself and for our neighbors, and the love, of which Paul speaks here, is the believer's 'yes,' in thought and feeling, word and deed, unconditional and without reservation, to that total claim of the loving God, insofar as it relates to the neighbor—a 'yes,' which is no human possibility but the gracious work of the Holy Spirit" (Cranfield).

sincere. Genuine, not counterfeit or showy. It is possible to pretend (even to one's self) to love others. John Calvin wrote: "It is difficult to express how ingenious almost all men are in counterfeiting a love which they do not really possess. They deceive not only others, but also themselves, while they persuade themselves that they have a true love for those whom they not only treat with neglect, but also in fact reject."

12:10 *brotherly love.* A second word for love is used here, *philadelphia*, denoting the tender affection found in families, now said to be appropriate to those in the church—which is the Christian's new family.

Honor. Since other Christians are in union with Christ, they are to be honored "above yourselves" because Christ is mysteriously present in them (Cranfield).

12:11 *fervor.* This Greek word is also used of water which is boiling (or of metal, like copper, which is glowing red-hot).

12:12 What makes it possible to endure affliction is joyful hope in one's inheritance in the age to come, coupled with daily, continuous prayer.

12:13 To be renewed is not just an interior matter of mind and emotions, but involves concrete outer action such as giving to those in need.

12:14–21 The emphasis here is on the Christian's relationship to those outside the church.

12:14 "Not only to refrain from desiring that harm should come to those who are persecuting us, but to desire good to them and to show that this desire is no mere pretense by actually praying for God's blessing upon them (it should be remembered that blessing and cursing are very serious matters in the New Testament as well as the Old Testament)—this is clearly opposed to what is natural to us" (Cranfield).

12:15 Believers demonstrate love to nonbelievers by being sensitive and responsive to their joys and sorrows.

12:16 Christians ought to provide a model of harmony for the world around them. Avoiding haughtiness, they ought to put in its place unself-conscious association with all types of people.

12:17 *Do not repay anyone evil for evil.* A common Christian teaching. See 1 Thessalonians 5:15 and 1 Peter 3:9. Christians are called upon to do not just what the consensus calls "good," but things that are inherently "good." These deeds will be recognized as such by those of good will.

12:18 *live at peace.* This is the normative principle in these verses. Christians are to work at creating harmonious relationships with all.

12:19–20 Seeking peace means doing away with the principle of revenge and continual escalation of violence. Using quotes from Deuteronomy 32:35 and Proverbs 25:21–22, Paul reminds Christians they are to leave judgment to God while they do all in their power to turn an enemy into a friend.

12:20 *burning coals.* Providing kindness of every sort to one's enemies may induce the kind of inner shame that leads to repentance, and hence to reconciliation and true friendship.

12:21 People who retaliate have allowed evil to overcome them. They have given in to their evil desires and have become like their enemy.

P.S.
If the next session is your last session together, you may want to plan a party to celebrate your time together. Save a few minutes at the close of this session to make these plans.

Loving Our Enemies

3-PART AGENDA

ICE-BREAKER
15 Minutes

BIBLE STUDY
30 Minutes

CARING TIME
15–45 Minutes

Will Rogers once said, "I never met a man I didn't like." Many of us would reply, "Evidently, Will never met so-and-so." If we are honest with ourselves, there are people in our lives with whom we can't get along and whom we don't like. However, we are taught in Scripture to love all people, including our enemies.

The thought of loving someone who divorced us, cut us out of a business deal, told rumors about us, or hurt us in some way seems beyond our abilities. What does the Bible really say about loving our enemies?

This may be the most difficult area of relationships for us to work on. It's bad enough that we have to admit we have enemies. But the idea of working with them and building relationships with them may be beyond what we can realistically deal with on a daily basis.

> **LEADER: Read the bottom part of page M8 in the center section concerning future mission possibilities for your group. Save plenty of time for the evaluation and future planning during the Caring Time. You will need to be prepared to lead this important discussion.**

In the Option 1 Study (from Matthew's Gospel), Jesus teaches us what it means to truly love our enemies. And in the Option 2 Study (from Paul's letter to the Philippians), we will discover Paul's teaching on unconditional love, which he experienced and shared while in prison.

Ice-Breaker / 15 Minutes

You Remind Me Of ... Write your name on a slip of paper and put it in a hat. Let everyone in the group select a name from the hat, but don't tell anyone whose name you have drawn. Choose a national park or monument that best describes the person you have selected. When everyone is finished, read out loud what you chose and see if the group can guess who you are describing.

GRAND CANYON NATIONAL PARK: What an impressive vista! You have character that has taken years of patience and constant attention.

GOLDEN GATE NATIONAL PARK: You bring people together and bridge the gap in a beautiful, stunning way.

SEQUOIA NATIONAL PARK: Your growth is so impressive that you reach into the skies and provide shade and security for many.

YOSEMITE NATIONAL PARK: You are the most popular choice for an exciting and adventurous experience!

MAMMOTH CAVE NATIONAL PARK: With miles of underground passageways, you epitomize depth, mystery and hidden treasures.

STATUE OF LIBERTY NATIONAL MONUMENT: You are a living symbol to those around you of freedom, hope and a new life.

MOUNT RUSHMORE: You are an enduring testimony to leadership, character and integrity.

YELLOWSTONE NATIONAL PARK: With your hot springs and geysers, you are a source of warmth for those who get close to you.

MOUNT RAINIER NATIONAL PARK: You keep people looking up, and your high standards can be seen from a great distance.

Bible Study / 30 Minutes

Option 1 / Gospel Study

Matthew 5:38–48 / Some People

Jesus totally rejects the thought of personal revenge, and calls instead for nonretaliation. Read Matthew 5:38–48 and discuss your responses to the following questions with your group.

38"You have heard that it was said, 'Eye for eye, and tooth for tooth.' 39But I tell you, Do not resist an evil person. If someone strikes you on the right cheek, turn to him the other also. 40And if someone wants to sue you and take your tunic, let him have your cloak as well. 41If someone forces you to go one mile, go with him two miles. 42Give to the one who asks you, and do not turn away from the one who wants to borrow from you.

43"You have heard that it was said, 'Love your neighbor and hate your enemy.' 44But I tell you: Love your enemies and pray for those who persecute you, 45that you may be sons of your Father in heaven. He causes his sun to rise on the evil and the good, and sends rain on the righteous and the unrighteous. ⁴⁶If you love those who love you, what reward will you get? Are not even the tax collectors doing that? ⁴⁷And if you greet only your brothers, what are you doing more than others? Do not even pagans do that? ⁴⁸Be perfect, therefore, as your heavenly Father is perfect."

"Returning hate for hate multiplies hate, adding deeper darkness to a night already devoid of stars."
—Martin Luther King, Jr.

1. Finish this sentence: "If Christians were to take this passage seriously, it would ..."
- ❏ put all of the lawyers out of business.
- ❏ put the banks and lending institutions out of business.
- ❏ get us all in better physical shape by going the extra mile.
- ❏ allow crime to run rampant.
- ❏ make us crazy by trying to be perfect.
- ❏ change lives like no rehabilitation program ever has before.
- ❏ make the world a safer and more peaceful place.

2. In this passage, Jesus gives standards of conduct for life which ...
- ❏ I will never achieve.
- ❏ I want to strive toward.
- ❏ I must attain before I can receive God's mercy.
- ❏ aren't actually standards, but are simply moral ideals.
- ❏ are perspectives I should develop as a recipient of God's mercy.
- ❏ other:_____

3. On the following moral issues, put an *"X"* on the scale according to which position is closest to yours:

ON REVENGE:
Call in "Rambo."   Immediately forgive and forget.

ON CRIME:
Call in "Dirty Harry."   Change lives through love and opportunity.

ON WAR:
Call me a "hawk."   Call me a "dove."

ON LAWSUITS:
Sue their socks off.   We can settle things if we just talk.

4. How did your parents resolve conflicts between you and your siblings?
- ❏ let us fight it out
- ❏ prayed about it
- ❏ yelled at us
- ❏ ignored it
- ❏ sat us down to talk about it
- ❏ took sides
- ❏ sent us out of the house
- ❏ other:_____

5. How do you generally deal with a broken relationship?
- ❏ have it out
- ❏ give the silent treatment
- ❏ write a letter
- ❏ make up quickly
- ❏ other:_____

6. Which of these "enemies" would you have a hard time loving?
- ❏ anyone from the IRS
- ❏ my ex-spouse
- ❏ my spouse's ex-spouse
- ❏ those I fought in war
- ❏ persons of a different race
- ❏ a rival at work
- ❏ liberals
- ❏ conservatives
- ❏ other:_____

7. Who in your life do you have to say "I'm sorry" to the most?
- ❏ parents
- ❏ siblings
- ❏ kids
- ❏ friends
- ❏ spouse
- ❏ rival
- ❏ coworker
- ❏ neighbors
- ❏ God
- ❏ other:_____

8. Who is someone to whom you need to work on showing God's love? What is a practical way you can do this?

9. When you leave this session today, how will you respond to the radical demands of this passage?
- ❏ conveniently forget it, like I've always done before
- ❏ struggle with it, but in the end stay with my relational patterns
- ❏ make some changes, but perhaps not all that this demands
- ❏ shoot for it all—turn my life around with unconditional love

COMMENT   In a world which focuses and thrives on competition, Jesus' words are a stark contrast. The world lives by a Win/Lose paradigm. But Jesus calls us to a Win/Win way of life. We are called to cooperate with our friends and family, and try to get along with our enemies. Even the world is nice to people they like. But a child of God is called to love their enemies.

Philippians 1:12–18a,27–2:4 / Paul's Enemies

Paul wrote his letter to the Philippians from prison in Rome. Actually he wasn't in a jail—but was under house arrest. Paul was able to receive visitors and correspondence. He was, however, bound to a Roman guard by a short length of chain that ran from his wrist to the guard's wrist. It is not surprising that all the guards got to know Paul and the Gospel. Read Philippians 1:12–18a,27–2:4 and discuss your responses to the following questions with your group.

¹²Now I want you to know, brothers, that what has happened to me has really served to advance the gospel. ¹³As a result, it has become clear throughout the whole palace guard and to everyone else that I am in chains for Christ. ¹⁴Because of my chains, most of the brothers in the Lord have been encouraged to speak the word of God more courageously and fearlessly.

¹⁵It is true that some preach Christ out of envy and rivalry, but others out of goodwill. ¹⁶The latter do so in love, knowing that I am put here for the defense of the gospel. ¹⁷The former preach Christ out of selfish ambition, not sincerely, supposing that they can stir up trouble for me while I am in chains. ¹⁸But what does it matter? The important thing is that in every way, whether from false motives or true, Christ is preached. And because of this I rejoice. ...

²⁷Whatever happens, conduct yourselves in a manner worthy of the gospel of Christ. Then, whether I come and see you or only hear about you in my absence, I will know that you stand firm in one spirit, contending as one man for the faith of the gospel ²⁸without being frightened in any way by those who oppose you. This is a sign to them that they will be destroyed, but that you will be saved—and that by God. ²⁹For it has been granted to you on behalf of Christ not only to believe on him, but also to suffer for him, ³⁰since you are going through the same struggle you saw I had, and now hear that I still have.

2 If you have any encouragement from being united with Christ, if any comfort from his love, if any fellowship with the Spirit, if any tenderness and compassion, ²then make my joy complete by being like-minded, having the same love, being one in spirit and purpose. ³Do nothing out of selfish ambition or vain conceit, but in humility consider others better than yourselves. ⁴Each of you should look not only to your own interests, but also to the interests of others.

1. As a child, who was the bully in your life? How did you deal with that person?

2. Does Paul sound like a person who is constantly in chains, awaiting the very real possibility of execution? How do you think he maintained such a positive attitude?

3. What is your view in difficult situations?
   ❑ Like Paul, I tend to see God's hand in my difficult circumstances.
   ❑ I occasionally see God's hand in my difficult circumstances.
   ❑ I think Satan is responsible for difficulties in my life.
   ❑ Difficult circumstances strengthen my faith.
   ❑ Difficult circumstances are a sign of unconfessed sin in my life.
   ❑ Difficult circumstances are a sign that I am doing God's will.
   ❑ When others suffer for the sake of the Gospel, I am encouraged.
   ❑ When I see others suffering for the sake of the Gospel, I get dis-
      couraged and think, "What's the use?"

4. What does this passage say about what your attitude should be toward Christians whose motives you might question?

5. What kind of struggles can a Christian expect (1:29–30)? How do you feel about being *called* to suffer for Christ?

6. What does it mean to consider someone better than yourself (2:3)? How does humility differ from being a doormat? Where has God been able to use bad for good in your life?

7. Does someone oppose you, this group or your church? Do they frighten you? Should they? How should we handle opposition?

8. Who do you have the hardest time being "one in spirit and purpose" with (2:2)? (It's okay if you would rather not answer this question out loud.)

9. Which of the things Paul writes about would help you relate to this person better?
   ❑ recognize that problems can actually produce benefits (1:12)
   ❑ admit that the issues that separate us don't really matter (1:18)
   ❑ stop being frightened by him or her (1:28)
   ❑ see our unity in Christ (2:1)
   ❑ show him or her more tenderness and compassion (2:1)
   ❑ swallow some of my pride (2:3)
   ❑ give greater consideration to his or her interests and needs (2:4)

Caring Time / 15–45 Minutes

1. Take some time to evaluate the life of your group by using the statements below. Read the first sentence out loud and ask everyone to explain where they would put a dot between the two extremes. When you are finished, go back and give your group an overall grade in the categories of Group Building, Bible Study and Mission.

 **GROUP BUILDING**

On celebrating life and having fun together, we were more like a ...
wet blanket _____hot tub

On becoming a caring community, we were more like a ...
prickly porcupine _____cuddly teddy bear

BIBLE STUDY

On sharing our spiritual stories, we were more like a ...
shallow pond _____spring-fed lake

On digging into Scripture, we were more like a ...
slow-moving snail _____voracious anteater

◯→◯ **MISSION**

On inviting new people into our group, we were more like a ...
barbed-wire fence _____wide-open door

On stretching our vision for mission, we were more like an ...
ostrich _____eagle

2. What are some specific areas in which you have grown in this course about relationships?
❐ increasing my awareness of how important relationships are
❐ having a closer relationship with God
❐ feeling better about myself as a valuable person
❐ growing in my family relationships
❐ strengthening my relationship with other Christians
❐ stretching my perspective and relationship with non-Christians
❐ dealing constructively with "enemies" and with conflict
❐ other:_____

MAKE A COVENANT

A covenant is a promise made to each other in the presence of God. Its purpose is to indicate your intention to make yourselves available to one another for the fulfillment of the purposes you share in common. If your group is going to continue, in a spirit of prayer work your way through the following sentences, trying to reach an agreement on each statement pertaining to your ongoing life together. Write out your covenant like a contract, stating your purpose, goals and the ground rules for your group.

1. The purpose of our group will be:

2. Our goals will be:

3. We will meet for _____ weeks, after which we will decide if we wish to continue as a group.

4. We will meet from _____ to _____ and we will strive to start on time and end on time.

5. We will meet at _____ _____ (place) or we will rotate from house to house.

6. We will agree to the following ground rules for our group (check):

❒ PRIORITY: While you are in the course, you give the group meetings priority.

❒ PARTICIPATION: Everyone participates and no one dominates.

❒ RESPECT: Everyone is given the right to their own opinion, and all questions are encouraged and respected.

❒ CONFIDENTIALITY: Anything that is said in the meeting is never repeated outside the meeting.

❒ EMPTY CHAIR: The group stays open to new people at every meeting, as long as they understand the ground rules.

❒ SUPPORT: Permission is given to call upon each other in time of need at any time.

❒ ACCOUNTABILITY: We agree to let the members of the group hold us accountable to the commitments which each of us make in whatever loving ways we decide upon.

❒ MISSION: We will do everything in our power to start a new group.

Summary. Paul reports on what has happened as a result of his imprisonment. He points to three positive outcomes, all involving the advance of the Gospel: (1) The Gospel is being noticed by all sorts of people who might otherwise not have heard it (v. 13); (2) the Christians in Rome have become bolder in their own proclamation (v. 14); and (3) even though some of the preaching that is going on springs from wrong motives, still the Gospel is getting out (vv. 15–18). Paul then shifts his focus from himself (and a report on his situation) to the Philippians (and advice on how to conduct themselves during the difficult times they are facing. Paul first exhorts the Philippians to be unified (1:27–30). Then he tells them that unity is achieved by means of self-sacrificing humility (2:1–4).

1:13 *palace guard.* These men were the elite soldiers in the Roman army, the bodyguards of the Emperor. Because Paul had been sent to Rome for a hearing before the Emperor, they were given the task of guarding him. Paul's guards changed every four hours or so, thus he got the chance to witness to a rotating coterie of soldiers from the key regiment in Rome. News of who he was and what he stood for apparently spread through the barracks and beyond into official circles.

for Christ. It had become clear to all involved that Paul was in prison not because he was a criminal who had been arrested for a crime he had committed, or because he had dangerous political views. He was in jail simply because he was a Christian. Thus, his arrest had cast no shadows on the name of Christ (see Acts 25:13–27; 26:30–32).

1:14 Paul gives the second reason why his imprisonment had served to advance the Gospel. Because of his example, other Christians had become bolder in their own sharing of the Gospel, and so the message was being spread to even more people.

1:15 *some.* Although "most" (v. 14) of the brothers and sisters have been inspired by Paul's example to be bolder in proclaiming the Gospel, "some" have used his imprisonment as the opportunity to advance their own honor, prestige, or cause. However, Paul still considers these people to be "brothers." He may not like what they are doing, but he does not reject them as illegitimate members of God's family.

envy and rivalry. That which motivates these people is some sort of grudge or hostility directed against Paul. They did not like him and wanted to hurt him by their preaching. What lay behind this animosity is not clear. Perhaps they looked on Paul in disdain because he was in jail, seeing this as a judgment from God against him. ("If God were really on his side, then he would not have allowed him to remain in prison," they might have reasoned.) Or maybe they were jealous of Paul's role as an apostle and saw this as a golden opportunity to advance their own positions and prestige.

1:18 *what does it matter ... I rejoice.* There is about Paul a truly astonishing, magnanimous spirit which does not care for personal reputation (or who gets the credit) as long as the job gets done.

Christ is preached. The one fact that makes it possible for Paul to accept this situation—and in fact to find positive value in it—is that whatever else might be said about these wrongly motivated brothers and sisters, their message still centers on Christ.

because of this I rejoice. This is an unexpected conclusion to Paul's report on his imprisonment. One might have expected an appeal that they pray for him in his difficult circumstances or that they work to get him released. This exclamation of joy is not how most people would sum up the experience of being in prison. But Paul has learned to see his circumstances in the light of God's plan; and so what matters is not how comfortable he is but whether the Gospel is thriving—and since it is, Paul can rejoice!

1:27 *stand firm.* This is a military term which conjures up images of a phalanx of Roman soldiers standing back to back, protecting each other while resisting the enemy. As long as everyone stood his place, such a formation was virtually impenetrable. The Philippians, too, are in battle and must adopt this same singleness of spirit and mind (unity) in the face of their enemies whose aim is to subvert the Gospel.

for the faith of the gospel. The goal is not victory on the battlefield, but the preservation of the Christian faith.

1:28 *without being frightened.* Yet another rare word, used in the Bible only this one time. Its original reference was to horses that were timid and which shied easily. The Philippians must not let their opponents spook them into an uncontrolled stampede.

those who oppose you. Paul does not identify their opponents. But in verse 30 he says "you are going through the same struggle you saw I had, and now hear that I still have." In both instances, Paul's opposition came from people who were opposed to his life and behavior as a Christian. In Philippi, this opposition came from secular merchants who were angry that he had freed a slave girl from bondage to an evil spirit. In Jerusalem, the opposition came from religious Jews who saw Paul's Christian faith as a threat to Judaism. The Philippians, too, are facing opposition of the same sort. A group of Christian Jews were advocating a return to the Law with all its rules and regulations.

1:29 *it has been granted.* It is assumed that Christians will suffer. But this is not something one has to put up with reluctantly because suffering for the sake of Christ is a gift of grace. Suffering is a privilege that has been granted to the Philippians.

1:30 *the same struggle.* Paul alludes to two incidents of persecution known by the Philippians: the one in Phillipi on his first visit there (Acts 16:16–40) and the other in Jerusalem that resulted in his present imprisonment (Acts 21:27–26:32). In each instance, Paul's struggle was with those who were opposed to his Christian beliefs and practices. In both cases his opponents stirred up the crowds against him and forced the Roman authorities to take him into custody. It is important to note that Paul was not being persecuted by Rome. His persecution originated with opponents of the Gospel. The Philippians are also facing the same sort of opponents.

2:1 By means of four clauses, Paul urges the Philippians to say "Yes" to his request that they live together in harmony. They have a strong incentive to be united to one another because of their experience of the encouragement, love, fellowship, mercy and compassion of God the Father, Son, and Holy Spirit.

2:2 *like-minded.* This is literally, "think the same way." However, Paul is not just urging everyone to hold identical ideas and opinions. The word for "think" is far more comprehensive and involves not only one's mind, but one's feelings, attitudes and will. Paul is calling for a far deeper form of unity than simple doctrinal conformity.

2:3–4 The road to unity is via the path of humble self-sacrifice. Paul has already demonstrated what he is urging here by means of his selfless attitude to those Christian brothers and sisters who preach Christ out of "selfish ambition" (see 1:17–18).

2:3 *humility.* This was not a virtue that was valued by the Greek in the first century. They considered this to be the attitude of a slave, i.e., servility. In the Old Testament, however, this was understood to be the proper attitude to hold before God. What Paul means by humility is defined by the phrase that follows. Humility is "considering others better than yourself." Christians are to accord others the same dignity and respect that Christ has given to all people. Humility involves seeing others not on the basis of how clever, attractive, or pious they are, but through the eyes of Christ (who died for them).

2:4 *look not only to your own interests.* Preoccupation with personal interests, along with selfish ambition and vain conceit, make unity impossible. Individualism or partisanship work against community. Note that Paul says "look *not only* to your own interests." Personal interests are important (although not to the exclusion of everything else).